Heart Visions

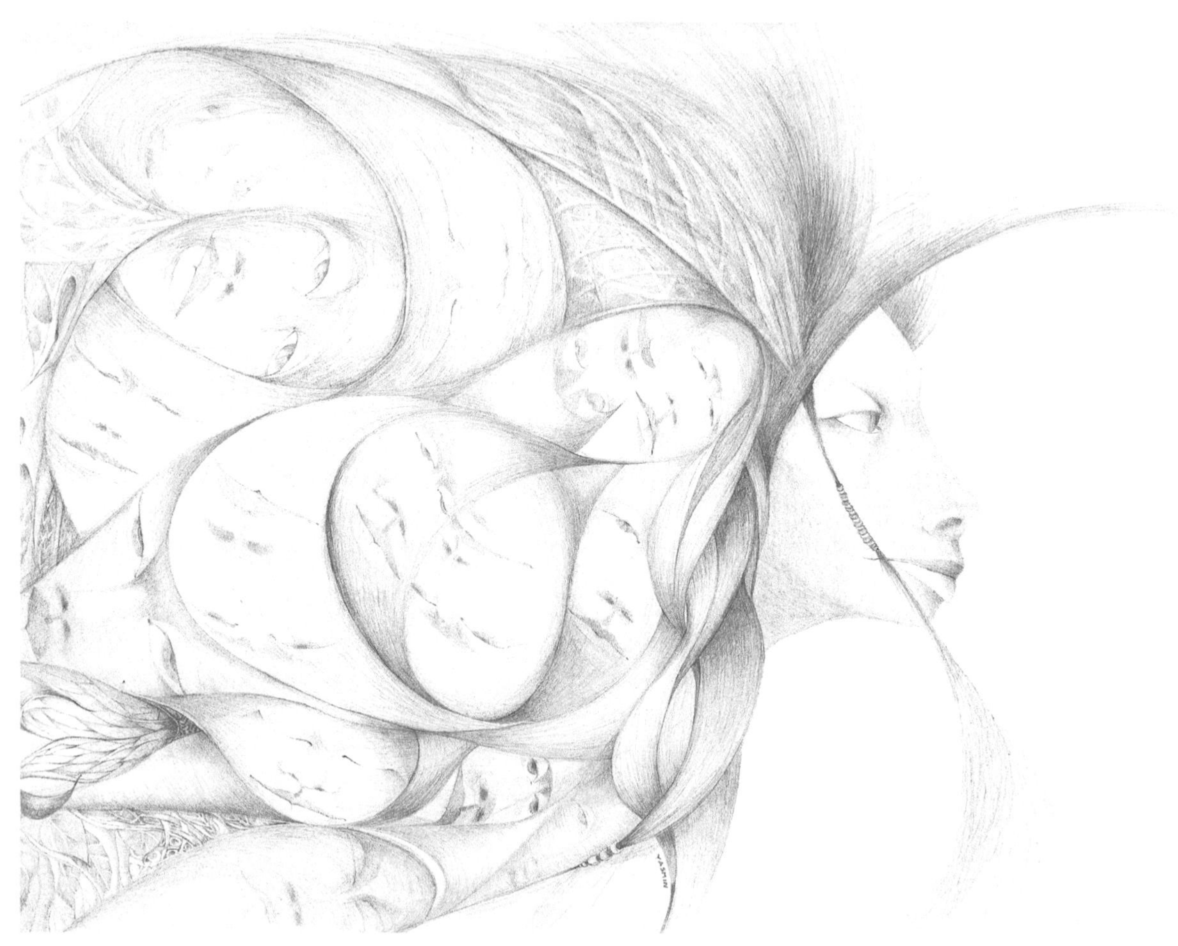

Self Reclamation: All of who I am and am to become

Heart Visions

Yasmin A. Sayyed, Ed.D.

PENTRONICS PUBLISHING

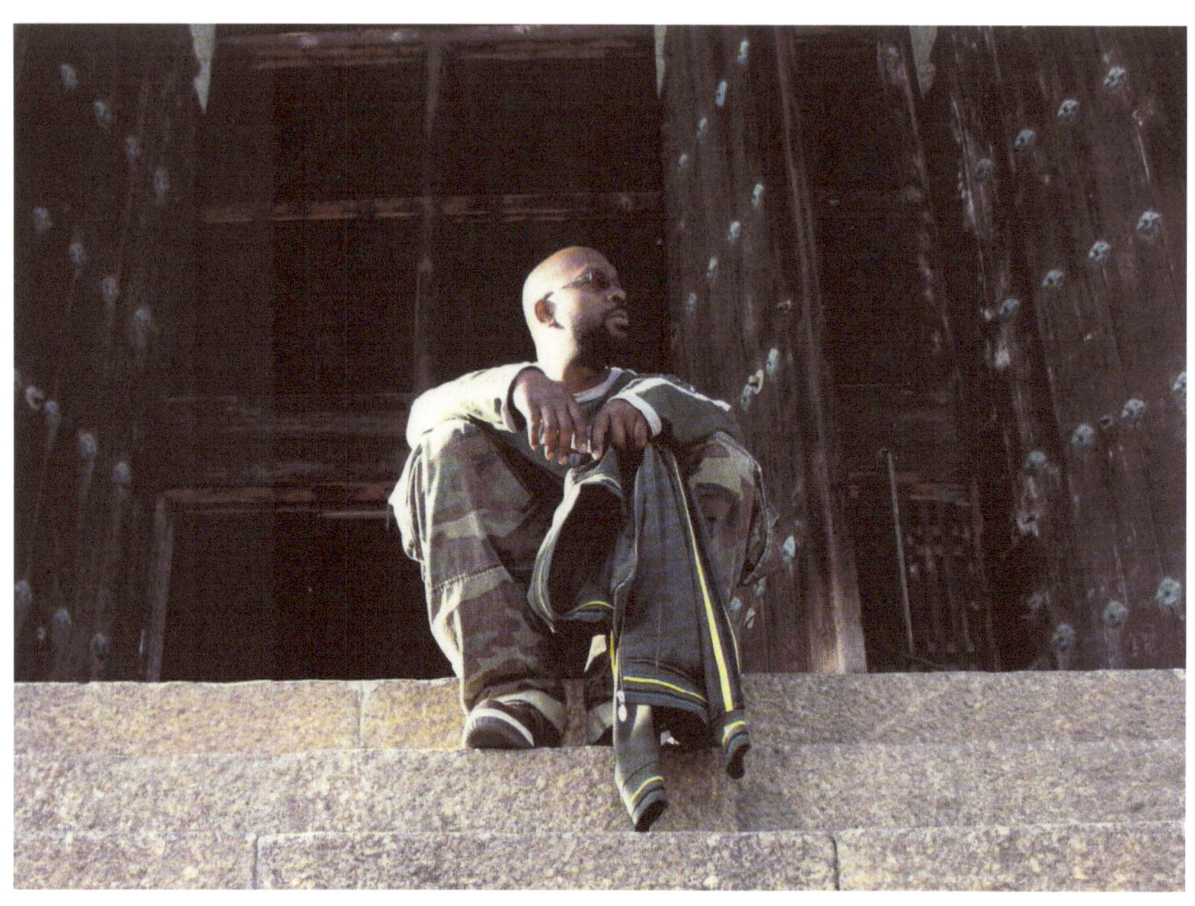

Taufiq A. Sayyed-Terry

December 24, 1972 - September 11, 2010

Artist's Dedication

This book is dedicated to the many people who have made its existence possible. Most eminently, my ancestors, those whom I can name and those whose names are beyond my consciousness, yet whose lens of perception and commitment to social justice I wear in my intellect and soul, and whose love of creativity resides in my eyes and hands blessed with the breath of *Spirit*.

This book is specifically dedicated to my family: to my grandparents who hailed from the Cape Verde Islands and Jamaica and who decisively laid the foundation for how I see and interact with the world.

It is dedicated to my sister, Kim, who as a young woman laboring under many years of domestic violence, took her own life—the loss of which informs my understanding of the intersectionality of institutional and interpersonal violence; to my son, Taufiq, whose existence serves as one of my greatest teachers, and whose infectious laughter helped me learn to smile again after his transition to the ancestors; to my elder son, Hakim, and my granddaughter, Imani, both of whom walk in creativity and consciousness and both of whom continually illumine decency, inspire hope, and engender clarity and tenderness; to my siblings, Big Hakim, Chuck and Zenny, whose love for me lies beyond articulation, and for which I am grounded in eternal humility and gratitude.

Additionally, this book is dedicated to all those who have known the wonders and heartaches of the profundity and breadth of living, and those who are agonizing under inequities, and who nonetheless raise pen and voice, paint, brush and movement in the causes of social justice and ethical behavior.

A separate note of appreciation is here noted for my friend, Lorraine Bonner, whose combined clarity of thinking and ethics inspire the same in me, and my friends Penny and Jack Shrawder, of Pentronics Publishing, whose technical expertise, spiritual hearts and unswerving belief in my work render *Heart Visions* a creative reality.

April 2015
First Edition, First Printing

Front Cover: *Watch Night Bird* by Yasmin A. Sayyed, Ed.D.
Front Cover Design: Penny Shrawder, Pentronics Publishing
Frontispiece: *Self Reclamation*
Interior Design: Penny Shrawder, Pentronics Publishing
Digital reproductions on pages 75, 113 - 127, and *Self Reclamation* on
back cover and frontispiece by Michael Nelson, GRAfx 8 Media Group, Minden, NV
Digital reproductions on pages 31, 67, 69, 71, 81, 83, 87, 129, 131, 133, 157
by Phil Stevenson, South Lake Tahoe, CA

Published by Pentronics Publishing
721 6th Street, Rio Rancho, NM 87124
PennyShrawder@gmail.com
YasminSayyed.com

ISBN-13: 978-0-9740915-3-2

Ordering Information
Order directly from Amazon.com

Books may be purchased in quantity and/or special sales by emailing the publisher:
PennyShrawder@gmail.com

Contents

Preface

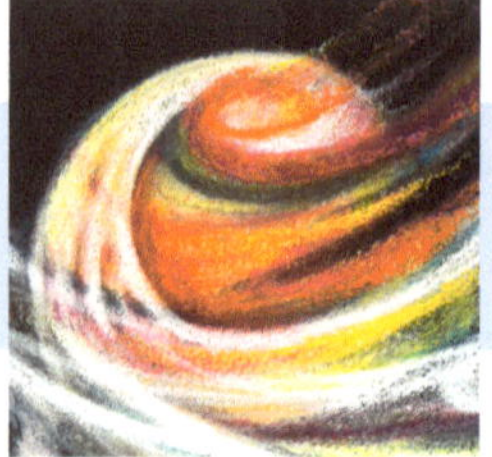 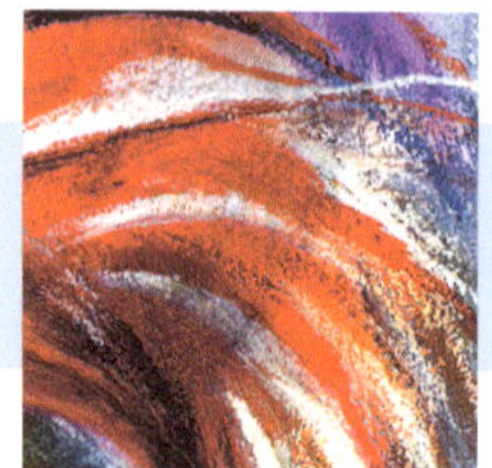 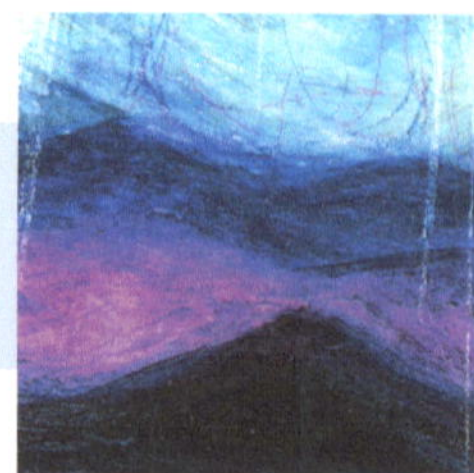

I have found when I listen, when I sit still and note what enters consciousness my art informs, it inspires and it salves; it leads and it follows in circuitous loops connecting and reconnecting sacred threads, and I, as artist, a living link in its process.

The arts can lead us from states of empathy depletion and civility decline toward the table of humanity and our seats therein. Art, as a language of the heart, can border cross and margins dissipate toward the universality of the specific and specificity of the universal, and toward a sensitivity to and solidarity with diverse human and nonhuman populations. May the meditations of my heart bear witness to its truth and illumine elucidatively that which upholds and that which hinders the development of knowing life fully, and that which upholds and that which hinders practicing social justice and honorable character.

My heart is called upon to witness truth, to note the flows of beatific and horrific life experiences, to aspire to do no harm, to dance in the magnificence and munificence of creating infinite possibilities, and to uphold and affirm the dignity of self and others.

Heart Visions is a visual and poetic presentation about fields of quantum leaps and exponential opportunities to dance in the perpetual winds of change. It is about the interplay of creativity and culture within socio-political realities. It bears witness to the depth and breadth of life, and a reflection of, and testament to the human spirit in the midst and aftermath of both blissful ecstasy and traumatic loss.

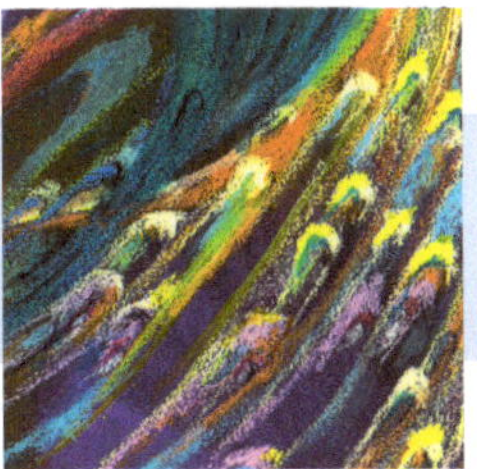 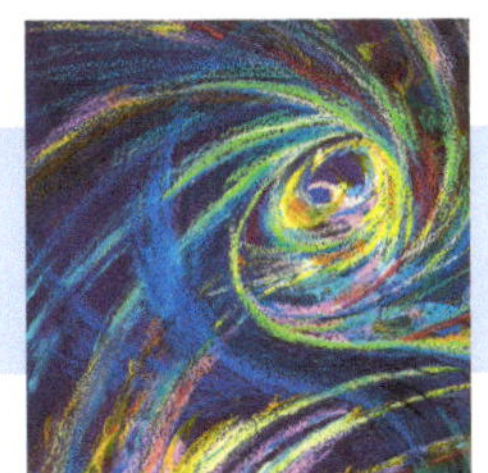 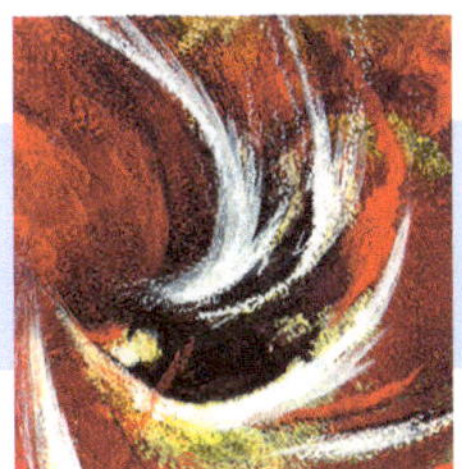

Ofttimes, I read or hear about forgiveness, and forgiving those who have trespassed and assailed against us, and have found myself pondering what life might look like, what our daily epistemological realities might be if we could readily apologize when and where we have trespassed and assailed, or where we as individuals and nations have benefited from such behaviors. What might it be if we could listen to those against whom we have aggrieved and/or speak with those who have aggrieved our psyches, our bodies, our communities, our nations, etc.? What gifts might we afford generations to come with models for authentic accountability with neither guilt nor retaliation?

The more thought I attended to the matter, the more in-depth an internal journeying I found my paintings involved, the processes of which deepened the significance of oneness with all that is and can be. From that place of knowing, an expanded awareness of the intersectionality of both grievances and joyfulness grew, and commingled with a deepened desire for social and political changes.

May uproars and gentle breezes move us towards heightened states of consciousness regarding our willingness to be on both sides of apologies and to resolve wrongdoings without needs for vengeance. It is my hope, it is my prayer and it is my concerted effort that therein peace may be still, and we know grace and divine character from the inside out.

Creating this book is an attempt to chronicalize my artistic journey from a heeding of internal calls towards an expansiveness of consciousness and commitment. Viewed are sixty-five annotated images arranged in thematic categories of the awakening, journeying, and embracing of life. It is my hope that my work delights the senses and inspires the soul.

Introduction

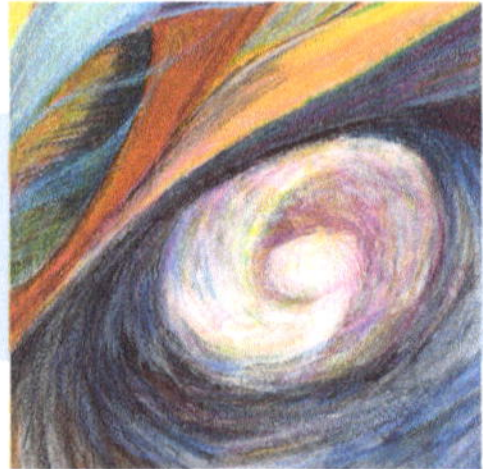
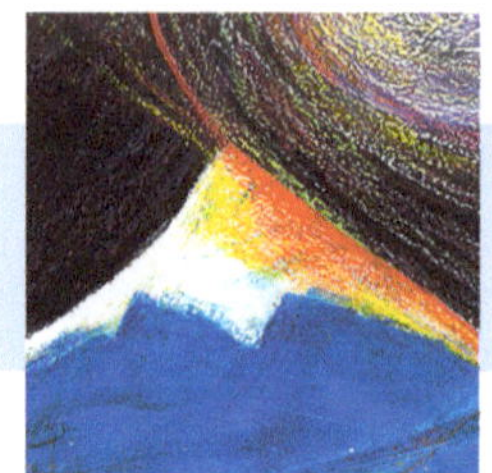
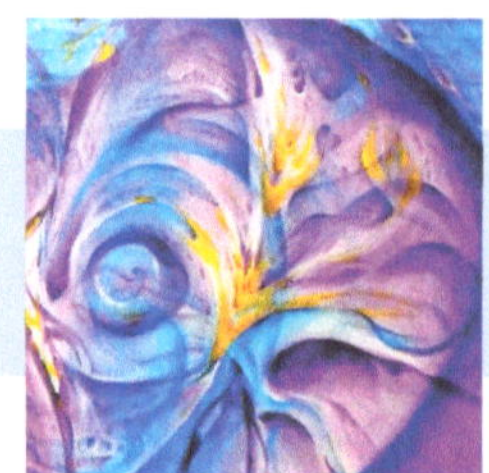

It gave me pause this writing about myself, my background, my entrance into the community of artists and those who inspired and encouraged. I wrote initially about my formal art training: competitive arts high school, undergraduate and graduate degrees in art, post-graduate training in clinical art therapy; New York Art Students' League; Harlem Arts and Culture programs; Harlem Black Arts Repertoire Theatre, and the long list of wonderful artists who personally touched my life and helped in the development of my belief in art as a self-informing tool: musicians like Kenny Durham, Reet Taylor, Julian Huell and visual artists like Bettye Blayton, Arnold Prince, Norman Lewis, and writers and thinkers like Bayard Rustin, Dr. John Henrik Clarke, Queen Mother Moore, El hajj Malik Shabazz, Mary Kochiyama, and many others, each of whom afforded me time and attention to develop a worldview in which my psyche could stay grounded and sane. Other imprints, like Fannie Lou Hamer, Stokely Carmichael, Bob Moses, Lewis Michaux and James Baldwin entered my life for but a few hours on a few given days. The impact, nonetheless, is continually revivified through my work as an artist dedicated to hope commingled with agency, and resistance commingled with persistence.

I experienced challenges trying to pinpoint where and when and how I entered the world of art. Harlem was a community teeming with artists in the sixties, promising a renewed renaissance of Black intelligentsia. It was a community that touted its artistic brilliance in public and private neighborhood landmarks. The works of Augusta Savage,

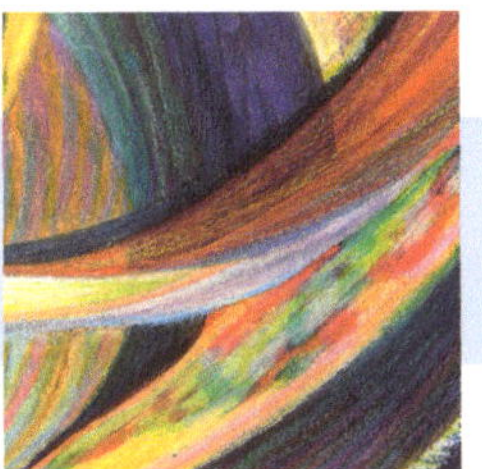 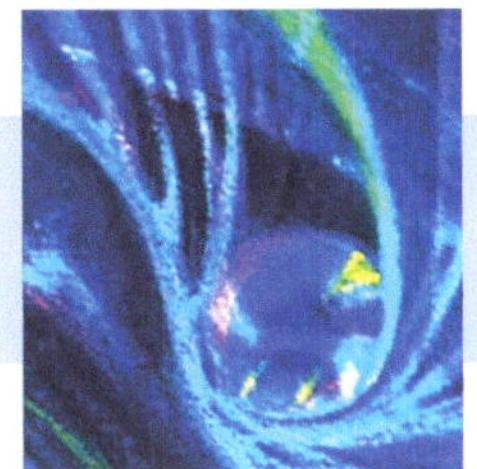 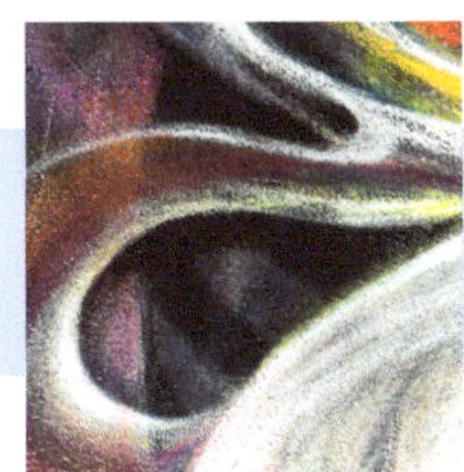

Jacob Lawrence, Charles Alston, Romare Bearden, were around us. Baba Olatunji and Mongo Santa Maria's drumming could be heard on the streets; Pearl and Percy Primus danced for youth and on and on. I, however, did not get to Manhattan until 1960, and I had already identified as an artist. Where, I pondered, lies the impetus of this honorific title, artist?

I started looking at how I have come to know the world and my place therein (epistemology), how I have come to be within the skin of my cosmological realities (ontology) and how I have come to develop and inculcate my values system (axiology). I approached the questions not unlike how I held leaves to the sunlight in profound and protracted observation of inside/outside cathexis.

I started meditating daily, and journaling what came up, and taking into contemplations questions of purpose and indivisibility, and where indivisibility meets and addresses inequities as well as blissful awe.

The arts, especially visual and poetic, have been my companions from those days to this very time. I know, believe and value through the whispers of the ancients, the practices of my immigrant grandparents, and the generosity of many. It is to them I honor with my footprints on this journey.

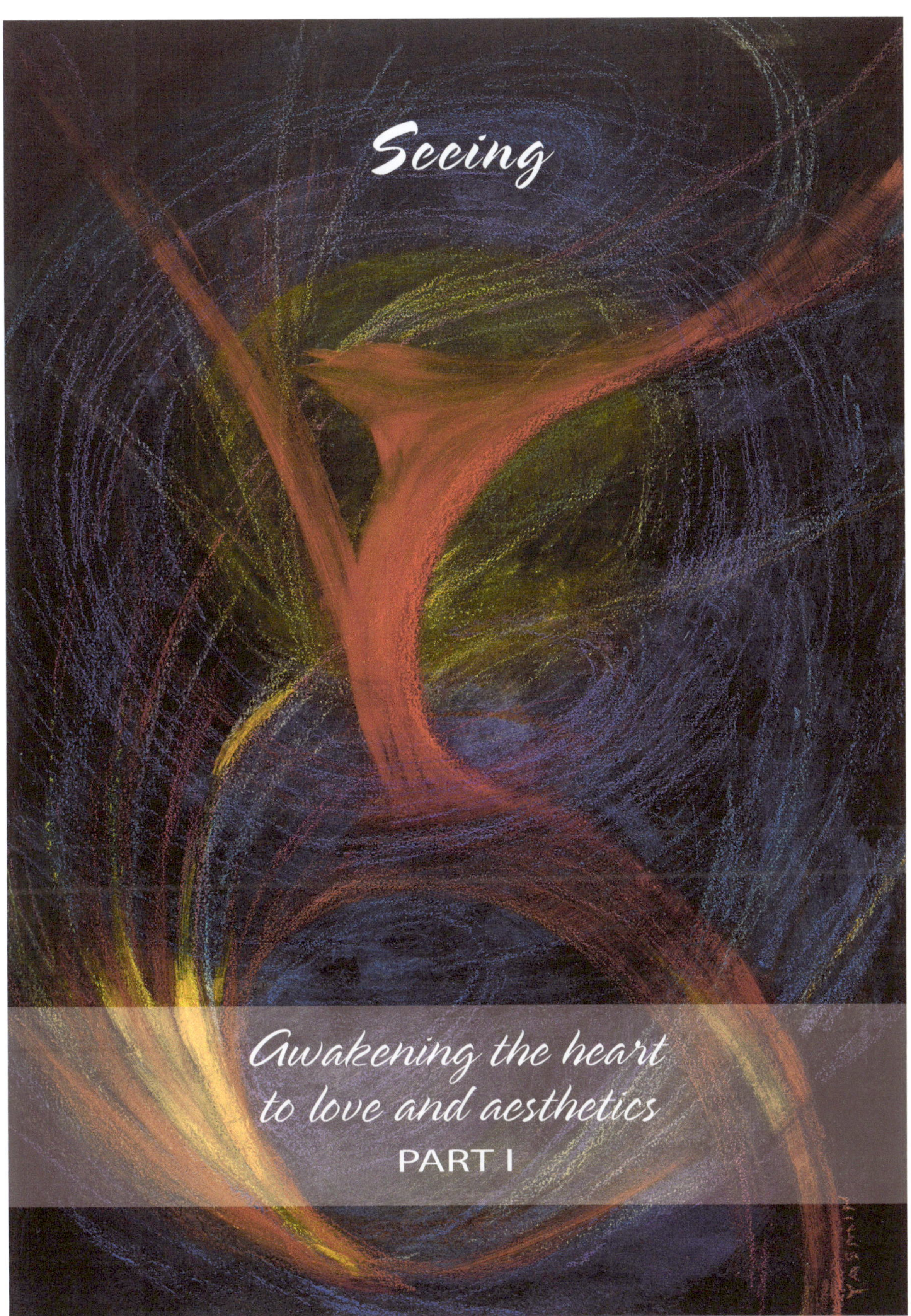
Seeing
Awakening the heart
to love and aesthetics
PART I

Seeing with the Eye of the Heart

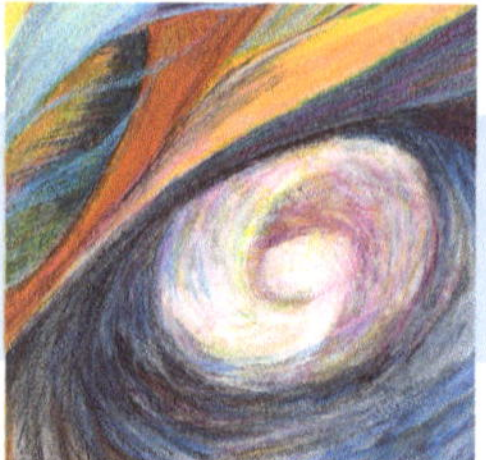
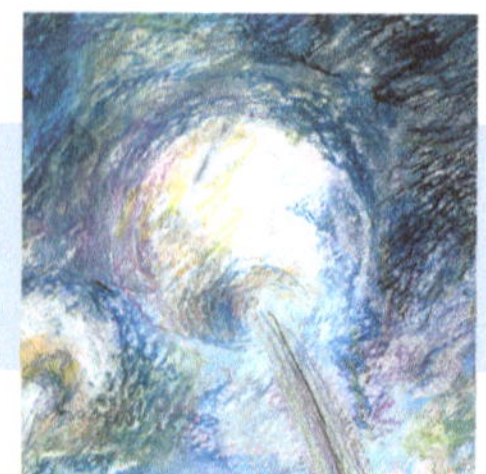
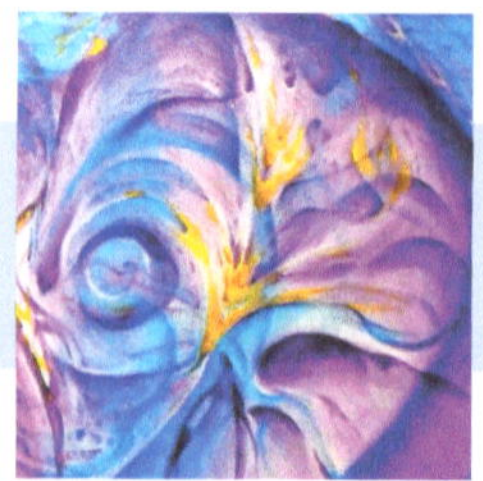

Knowledge is better than riches —African proverb

In fierce moving and gentle winds, change bows.
To ferocious turbulence and tender breaths of spirit, change bows.
Uproar and uncertainty abound in life and therein reside infinite opportunities for personal, societal and global change.
Turbulence, though not always readily understood, nor readily appreciated, presents opportunities to embrace character and interconnectedness as seen through the eye of the heart... heart visions

The poetic heart, metaphor for consciousness and compassion, tenderness and connectedness sees with a spiritual eye of inclusivity. This seeing with the heart requires not an obscured vision of existing inequities, nor one trained in the privileges of not knowing, but rather a consciousness of optimism commingled with actions toward fruition of authentic liberation. I speak not of toxic hope, which serves lemming-like belief systems and furthers injustices. Here, I am putting forth a worldview of discerning scrutiny, artistically expressed.

As a young child, I drew the world around me. I drew the orderly kitchen of my Jamaican grandmother. I drew the small table where I was expected to remember table manners before being integrated, and at times reintegrated, into the dining room scene of multiple utensils, plates and glasses. I entered the world of color, patterns, lines, textures and visual tension found in its brick and wooden walls, tiled floor, round shouldered ice box, wood and coal burning cast iron stove, wringer washing machine, and glass door cupboards. I learned a way of seeing life around me in minute details of organized patterns and organic designs.

My Cape Verdean grandfather and I would sometimes draw together. Sometimes we laughed uproariously. Sometimes we sat for long periods in silence, understood and appreciated; we communed. Our drawings, we put in the attic, in an old trunk, placed under

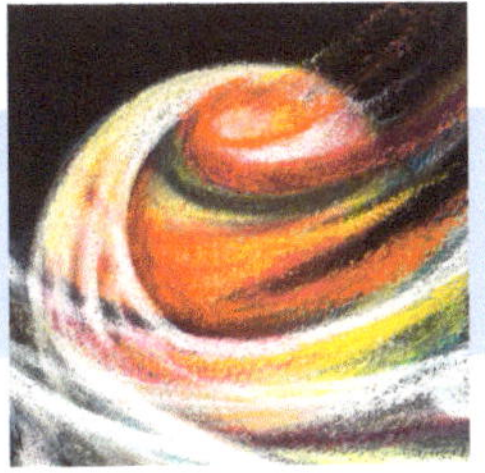
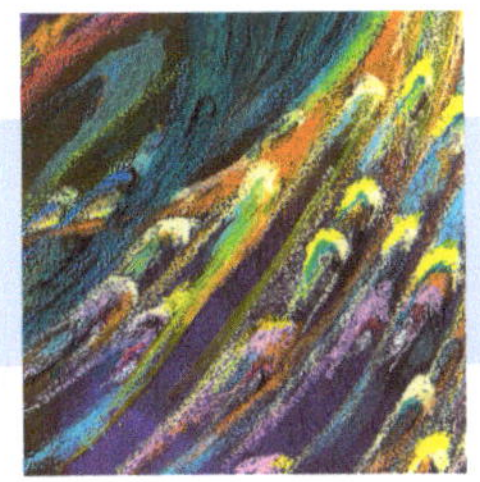
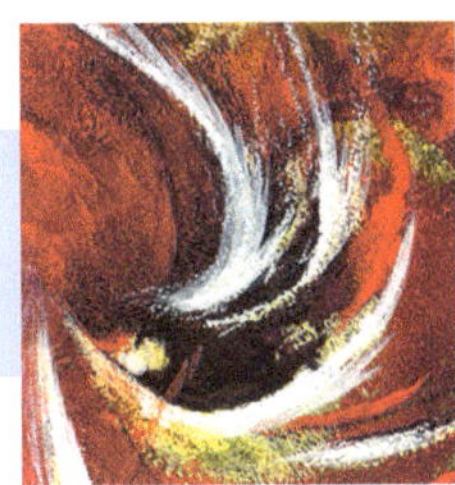

the circular stained glass window. There was a time with my grandfather in the woods, with playful light dancing and pausing, meandering and sauntering through the thickets, a time of remembered morning dew and promises of warmth to follow the nip of early day cling. It is my earliest remembrance of feeling indivisible with nature's beauty.

I was obsessed and mesmerized by the variations of colors and shapes, patterns and movements of all make and manner of things. I was transfixed by how elements interconnect and change one to the other. I was fascinated by how light passing through crumbled colored cellophane created its designs on paper and how sunlight passing through laced curtains patterned my grandmother's table linen. The translucency of a leaf held to a brightly lit sky, deeply-grooved cracked designs in dried mud, decomposing brick walls, swirling grains in tiger oak table tops, inverted images through a large magnifying glass, oil drops in rain puddles ... I looked deeply at everything, seemingly with great cathectic energy. How curvaceous and angular forms interplayed, how concentric circles and patterns within patterns in vegetables and fruit rhythmically and magically repeated themselves ... I did not then know about fractals but was enchanted by their presentations in my eyes and psyche.

I would lie on my back, sometimes in moist grass, holding a leaf in the hand of an arm stretched towards the sky. On brightly lit days, light traversed the leaf to capture my attention with its design minutiae. I would stare, and gently position and reposition the leaf in order to facilitate changing angles of observation. The veins of the leaf, with its interweaving patterns of simultaneous uniqueness and uniformity of forms and lines, intrigued the imagination. One day I slowly moved a leaf closer to my face; I stepped outside of myself and inside of the leaf, and it into me. There was no separation of form and being, no observer and observed. We were one. That feeling is what I hope my paintings portray. The force of consciousness that I knew that day, today I paint to bring forth messages from within.

Messages From Within

Silence bears the unwrapped gifts
awaiting our listening
the unstepped movements
towards being one with

acrylic and oil pastels
30 x 22 inches

Page 10

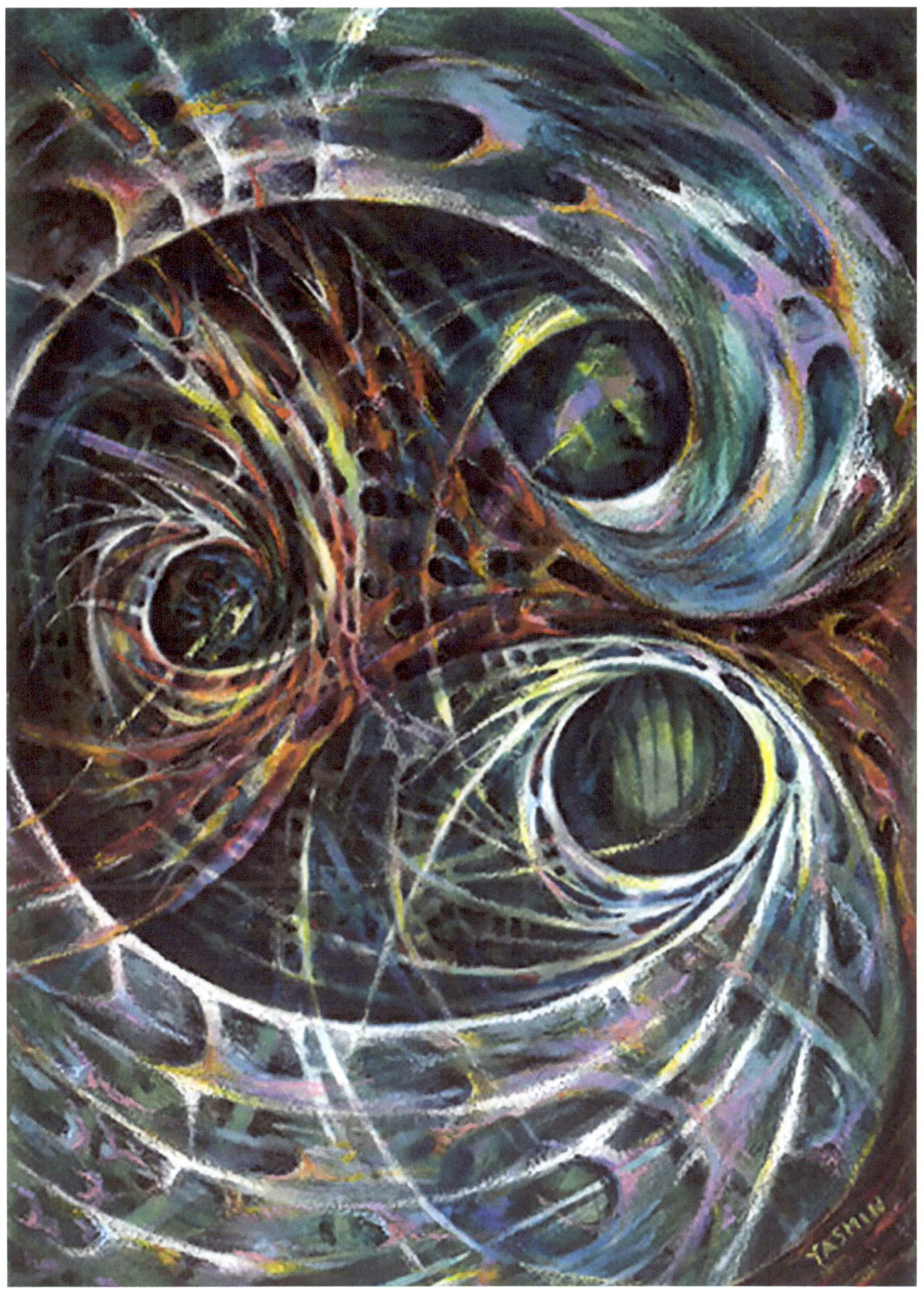

PLATE 1

Leila

Embracing life's organic flow
Pushing not
against the stream
Traversing rather
its flow of currents

acrylic and oil pastels
30 x 22 inches
collection of Margot Gibney

Page 12

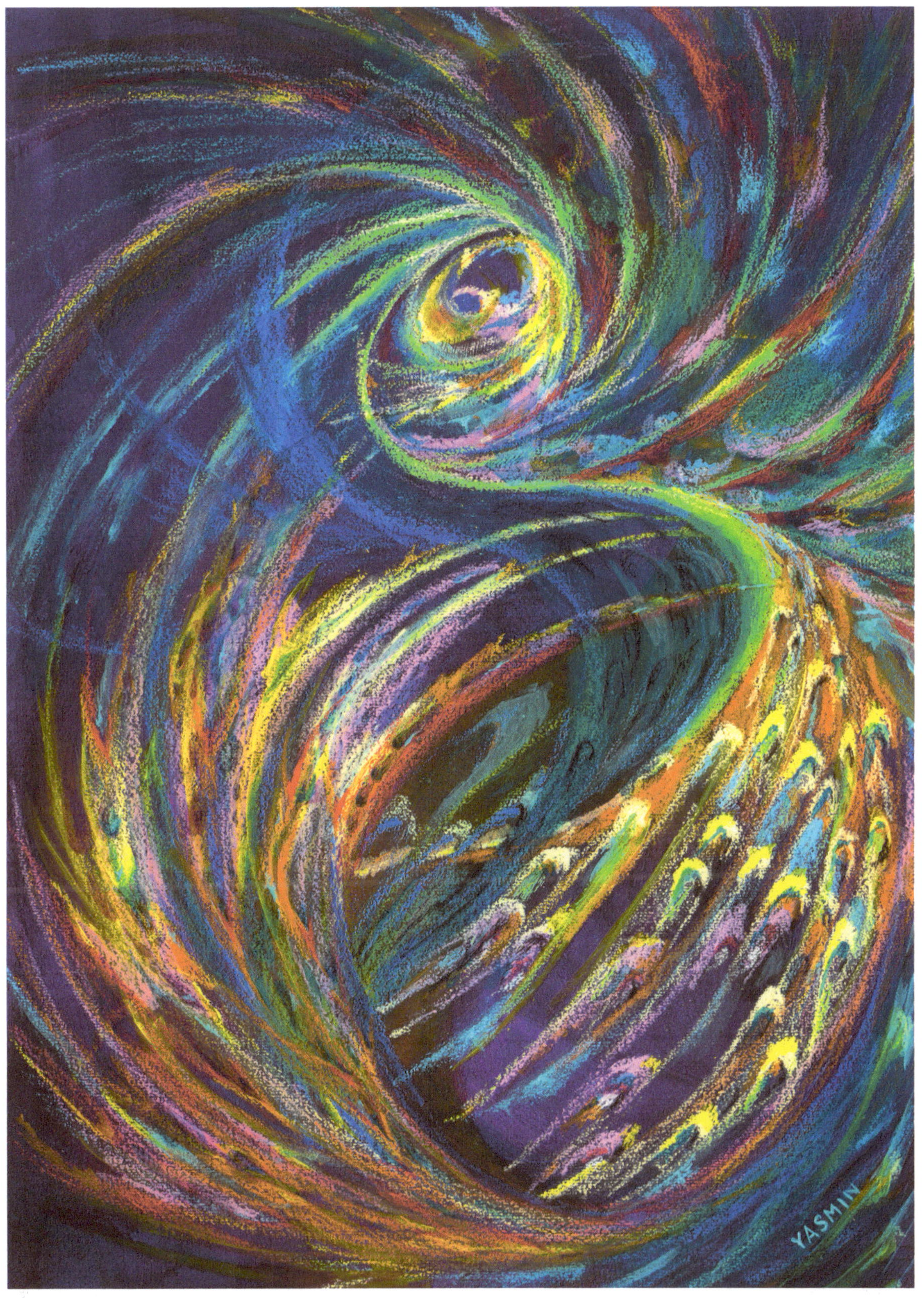

PLATE 2

Spirit Dancer

The world old and I young
It huge and I infinitesimally small
I dance the defies of time
and space
of form and matter
to simply be
one with
all that is, was
and has yet to become

acrylic and oil pastels
30 x 22 inches

Page 14

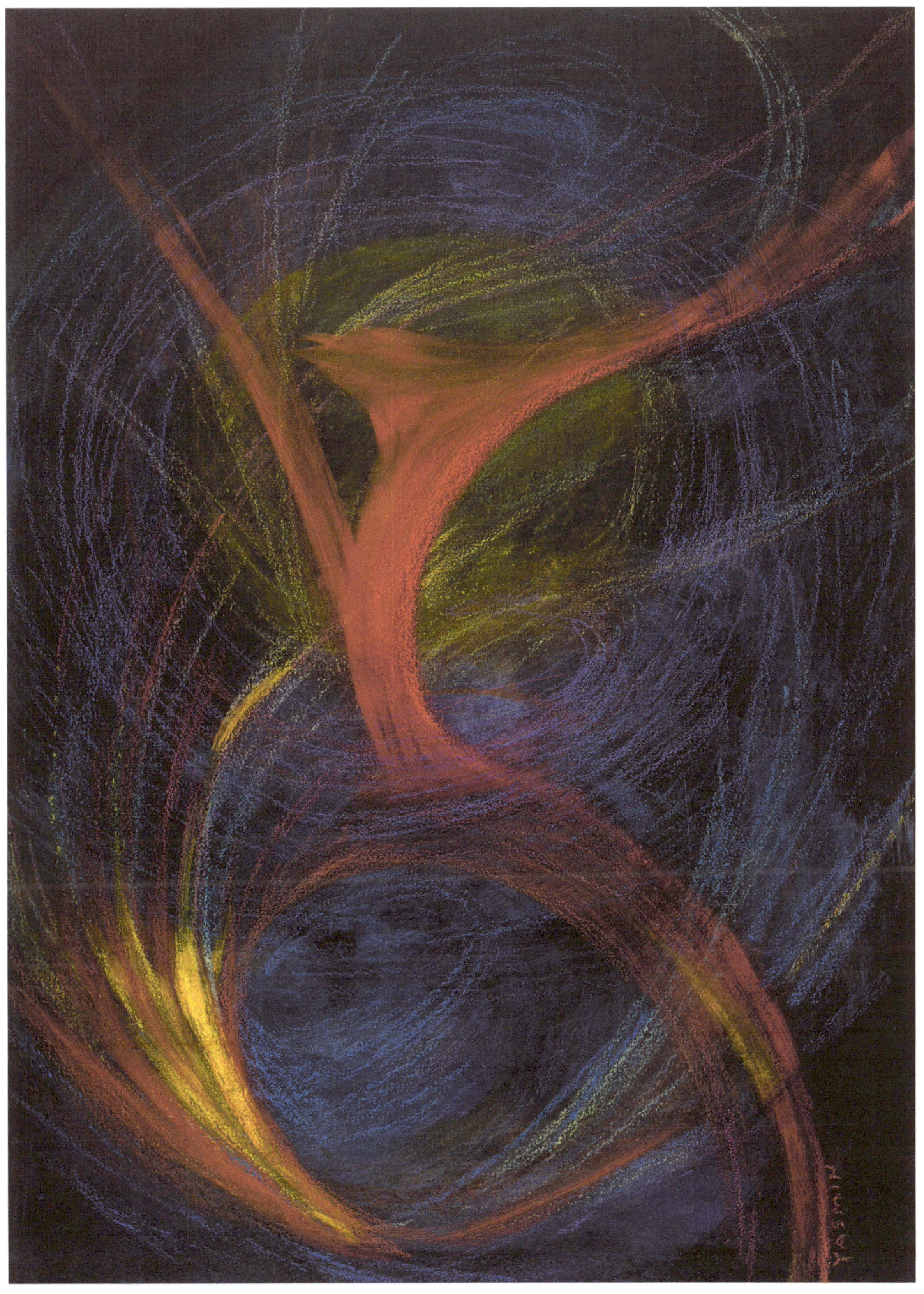

PLATE 3

Reflections

Enveloped and embraced
cradled and salved
crevices and abysses of
veiled consciousness are
rendered visible

acrylic and oil pastels
22 x 30 inches

Page 16

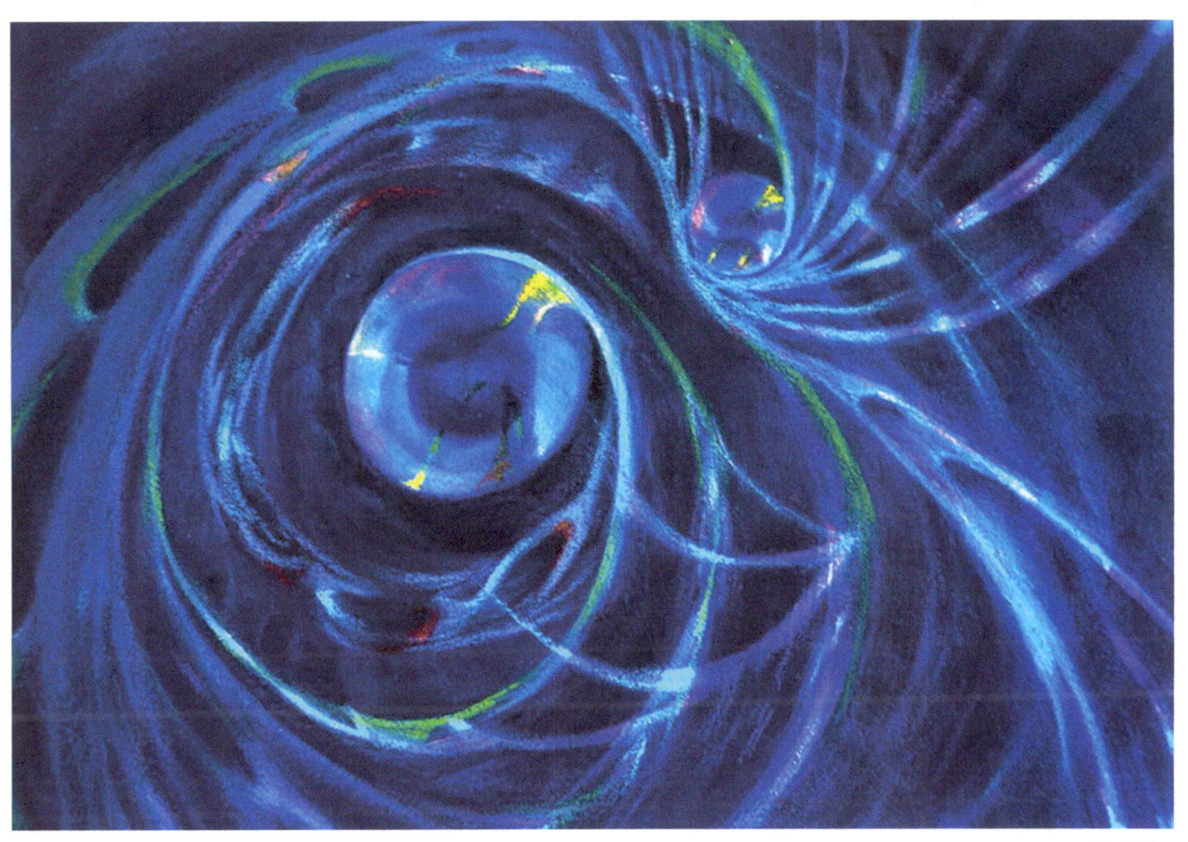

PLATE 4

Seeing at the Edge of the Cliff

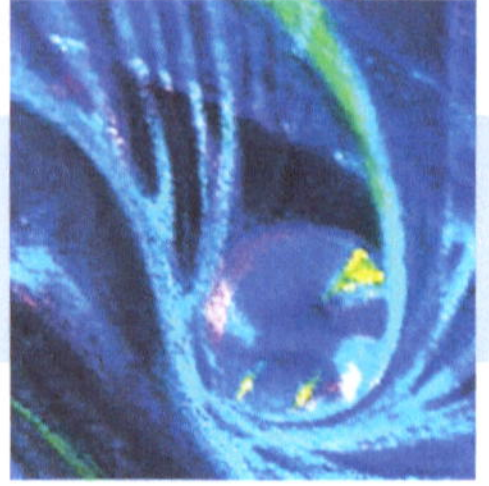

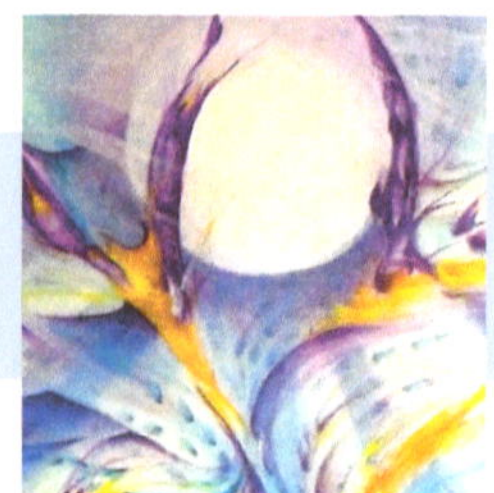

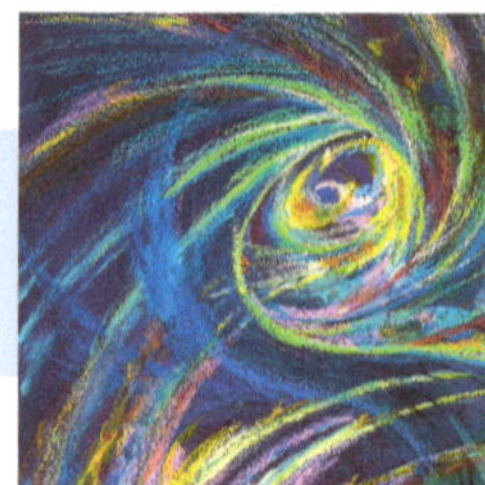

We climb the backs of our ancestors and stand on their shoulders
to see the world as we do today —African proverb

I used to spend many hours in the upstate-mountains of New York with my Cape Verdean grandfather. He would walk up to the edge of a cliff and praise the splendor that lay before him. He'd tell me to behold what had been created just to stir the artist within me.

One such morning I lay on the damp ground and looked out to behold the beauty of the mountains through early morning mist. "Come here," my grandfather beckoned, "See the majesty and quiet prayer of nature." By, here, he meant the edge of the cliff. I was scared. He'd have none of it. "Come," he said.

"All this is for you. You have nothing to fear from your gift. You cannot own it, but from those who walked here before us, we can borrow its majesty. We can wear it as lovers of divinity along a journey of becoming one. Come, see how magnificent is this veil of knowledge," he said, pointing to the canyon below.

Fear gripped me. I was afraid of looking over the edge, but more worried about disappointing him than looking into the deep ravine, so I dug my hands into the softened earth and slowly, ever so slowly, dragged my little body ... feeling my shirt bunch up, and the wetness of the earth slide along my bare belly. I stopped, caught the dew on my outstretched tongue, caught dampened earth-scents in my nostrils and dragged myself

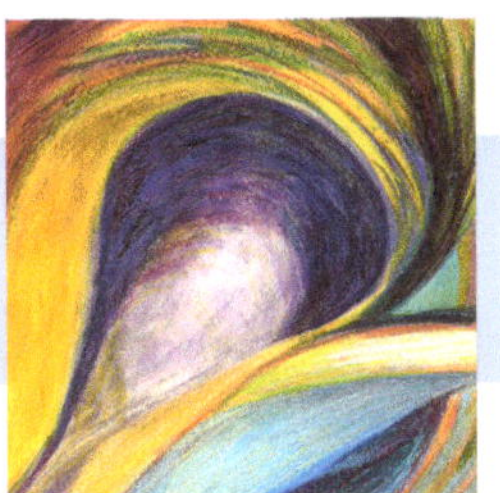 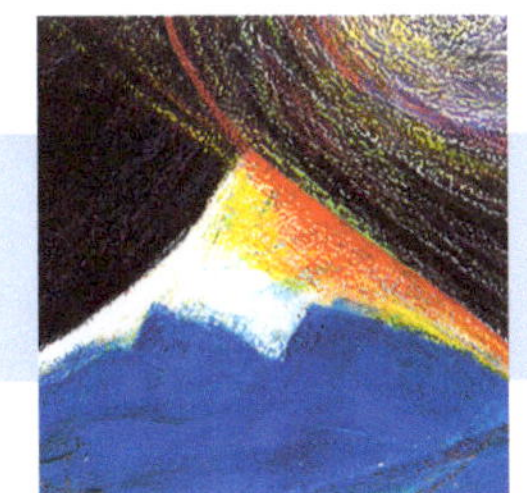 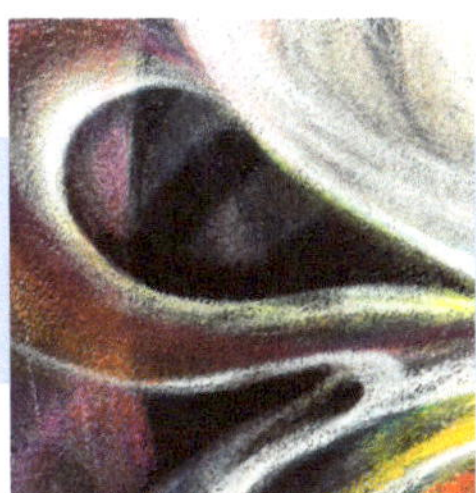

closer and closer. I let my tongue slide along … licking the droplets of grass … all the time trusting my grandfather and what was to lie before me as promised. The moss-laden tree-images slipped into the background of the hills, while the sun, not fully up, toyed playfully with colors and shadows as I inched closer.

Slowly, I made my way to the edge. At the feet of my grandfather, I looked straight out. Too timorous to move my head sweepingly, I allowed my eyes to move in the tiniest of increments from south to northwards, taking in the skyline of greenish-blue and purple-gray hilltops with rising sunlight dancing between tree and mountain ranges. My heart swelled. Tears welled up in my toes and ran along my spine. I looked down. Then up. Then down again, and around. I was awash with baby tears that spilled from my eyes, ran down my face and fell into the earth. With face cradled in my small hands … my cup runneth over and over.

> At the edge of the cliff with his words in my ears and in my heart … *trees stand tall, and birds fly because they, like the artist and the firewalker, believe they can….*
> I stood tall like the mountains, wanting to fly in the openness of the skies.
> Stepping back from the edge, I stood tall, and shouted, *Behold!*
> And with his spirit propelling my wings, I leapt, pranced and took off flying.

Quiet Prayer

Solitude in nature
awes and bonds
Affords ways of knowing
unspoken bliss
communed within the soul

acrylic and oil pastels
30 x 22 inches
collection of Melvin Terry

Page 20

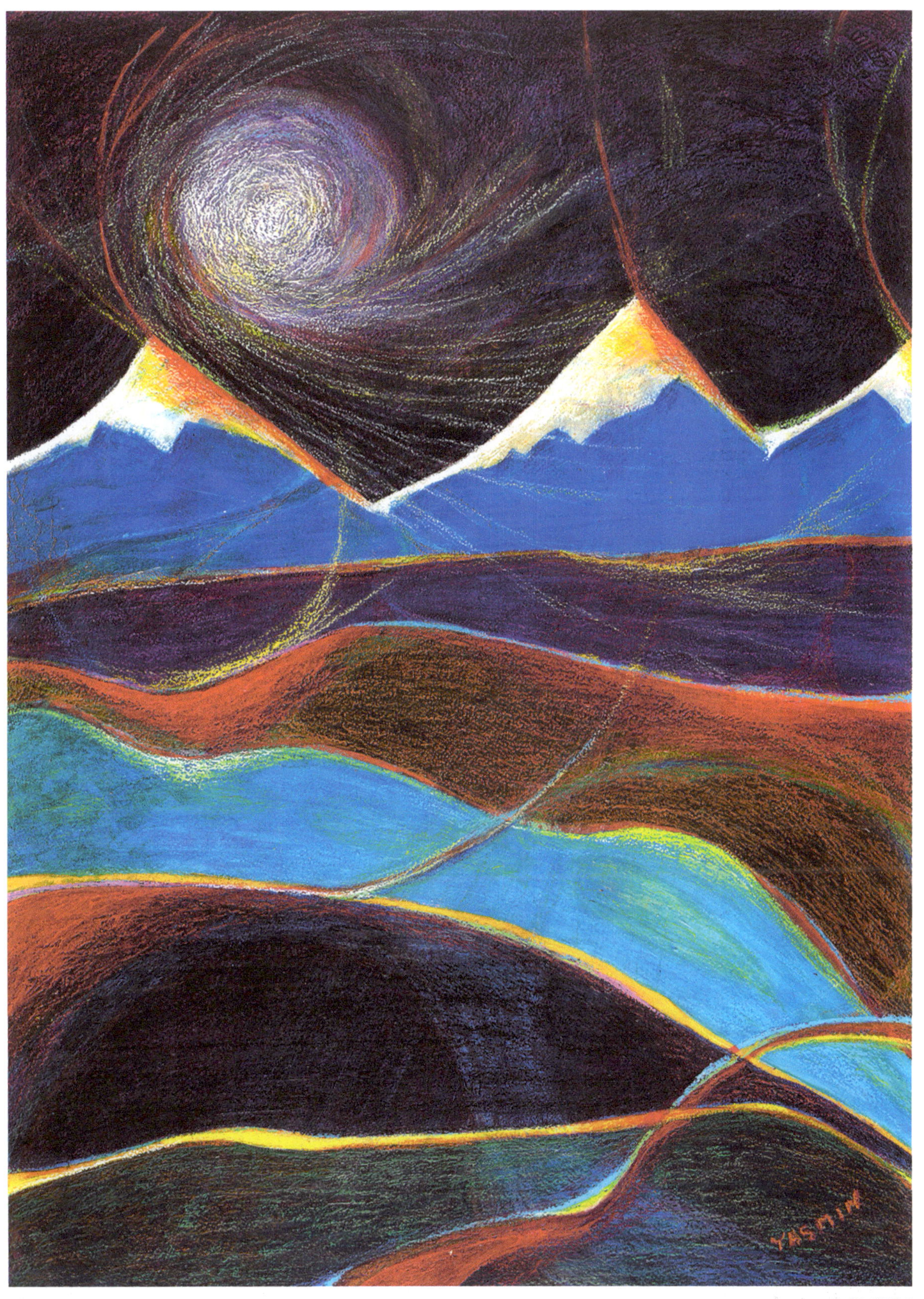

PLATE 5

Veils of Knowledge

Ways of knowing and being
believing and loving
Perceptions projected and assumed
inculcated and expressed
as we pass through veils of knowledge toward the
sacredness of educating the soul

acrylic and oil pastels
22 x 30 inches

Page 22

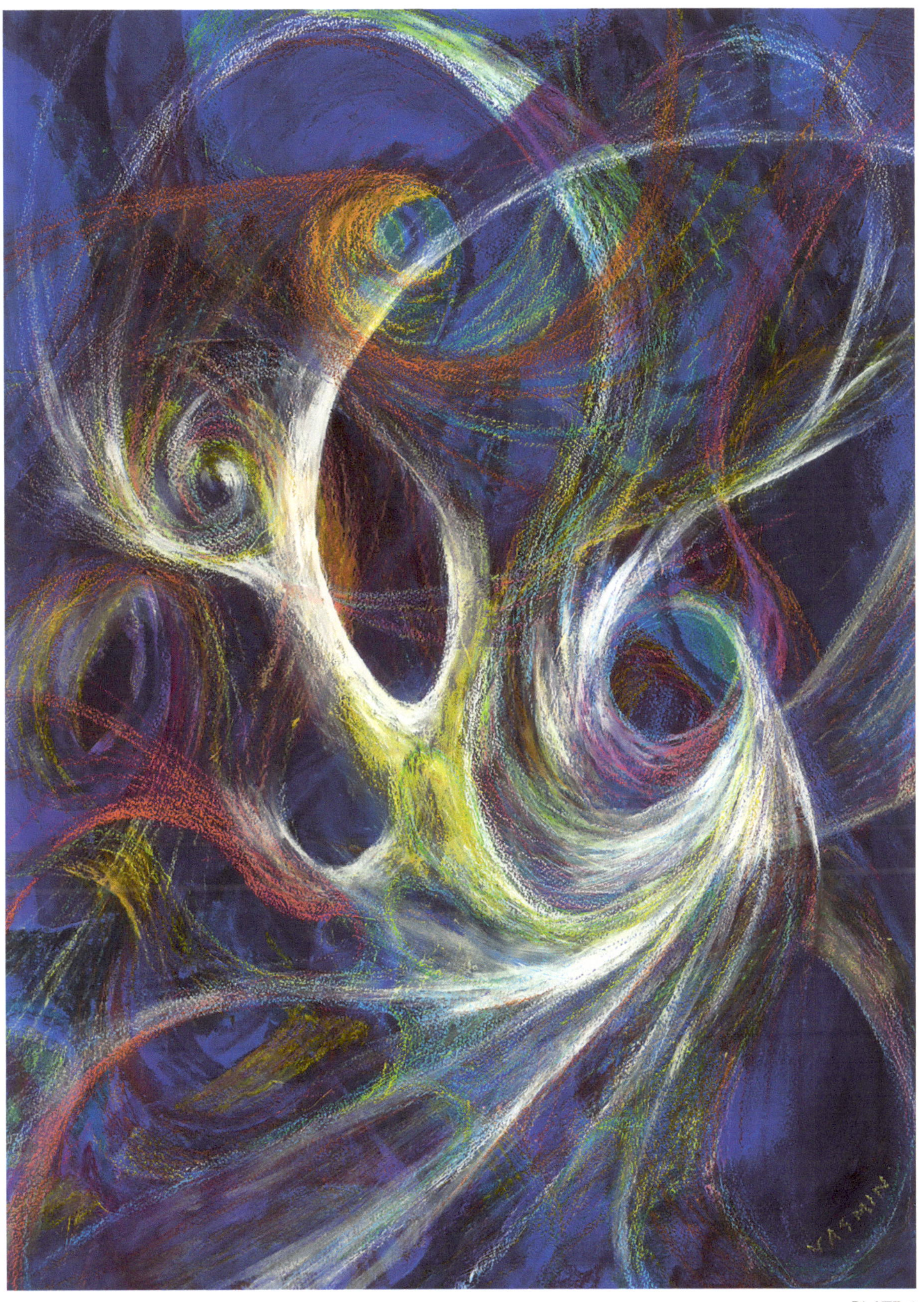

PLATE 6

Rumi's Guesthouse

Visitors come
welcomed, scorned, feared
Come
Joy, anxiety, chaos
Every connection
an opportunity
to dance in the fullness of life

acrylic and oil pastels
30 x 22 inches

Page 24

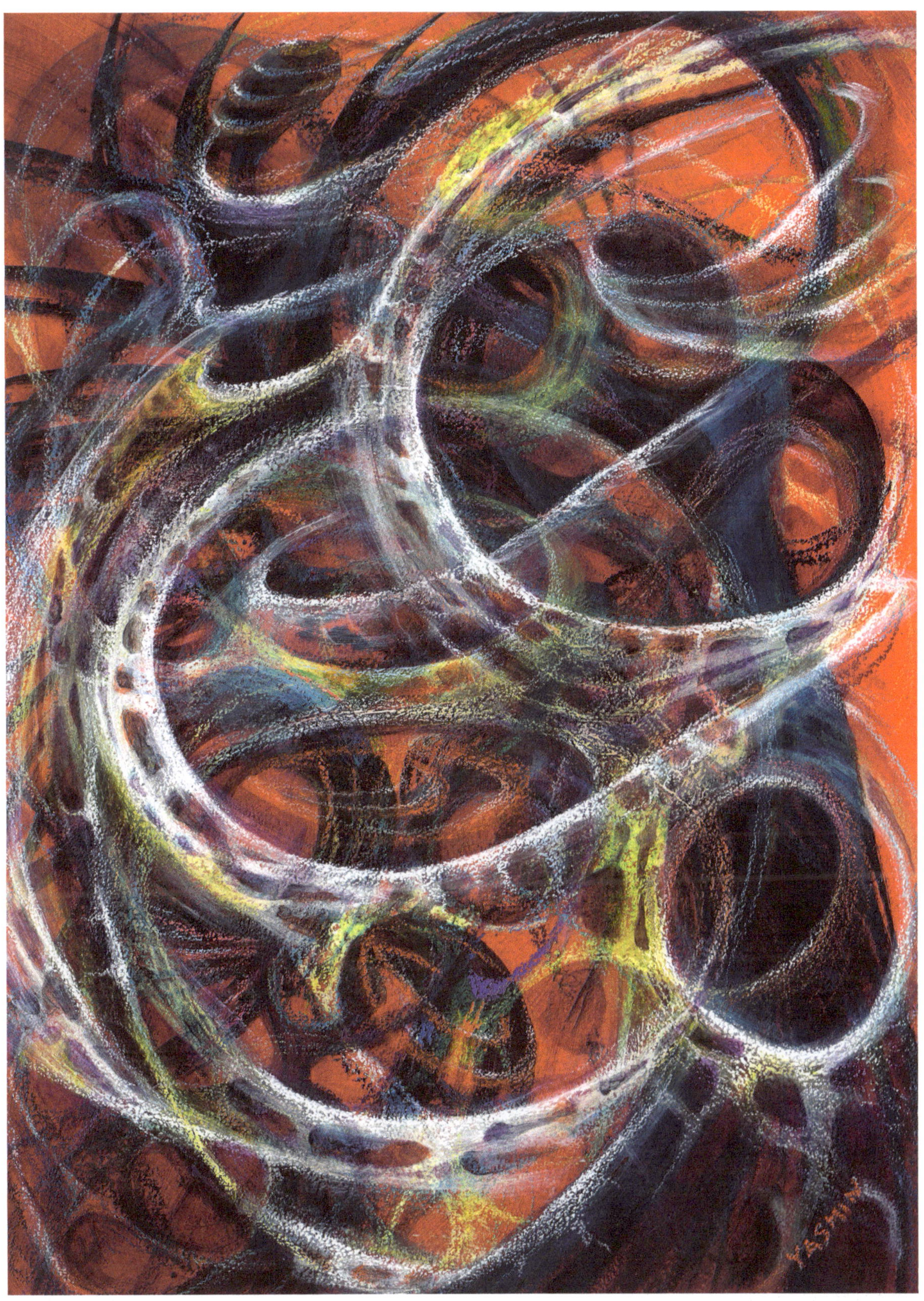

PLATE 7

Twirling Dancer

Twirling release of ego
in continual effort
to awaken the eye
to see

acrylic and oil pastels
30 x 22 inches

Page 26

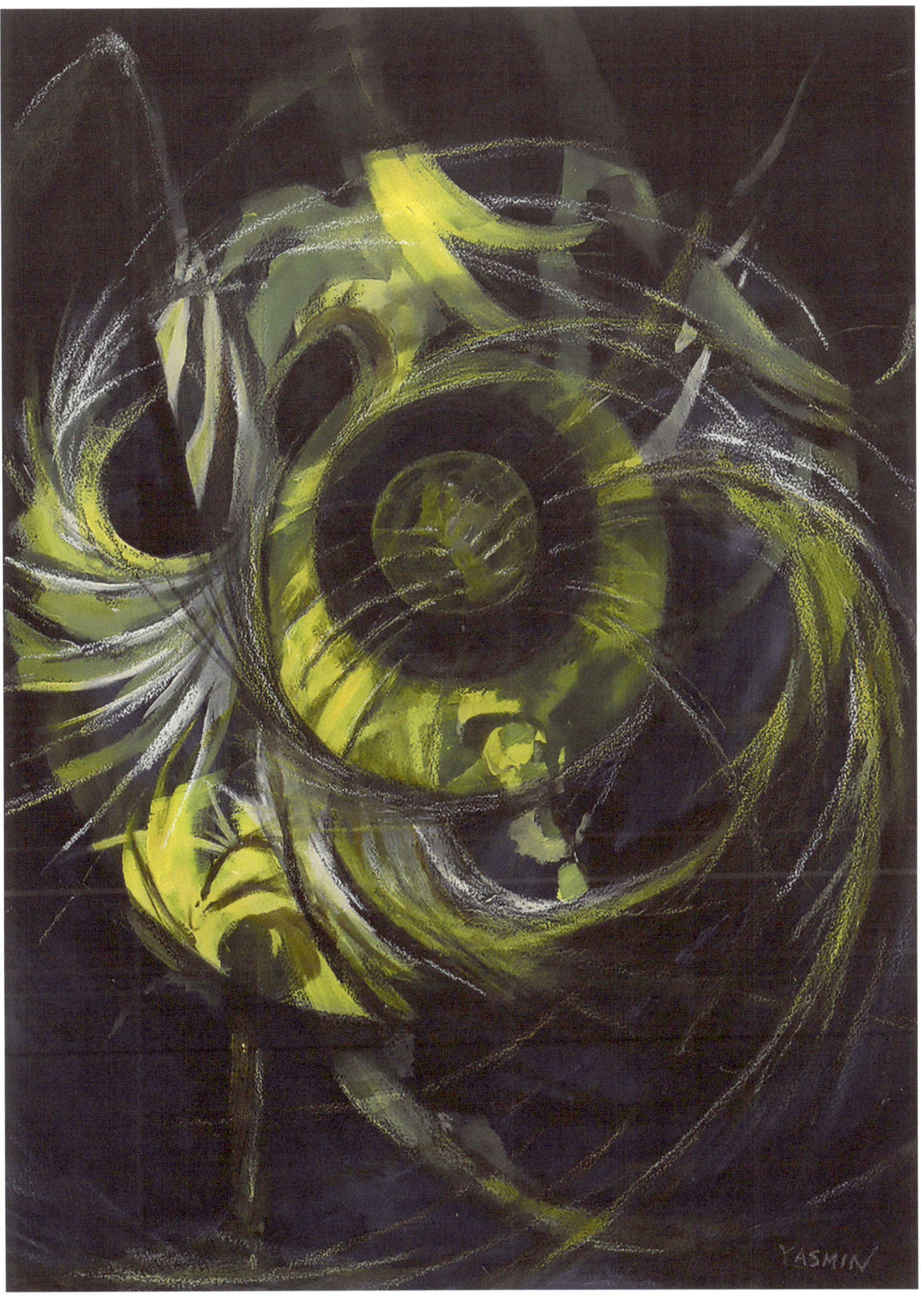

PLATE 8

Lovers Along the Journey

Beloveds holding hands and hearts
praising the sublime
In joined footprints
chant poems in love
of *Thee*

acrylic and oil pastels
30 x 22 inches
collection of Leah Rescate

Page 28

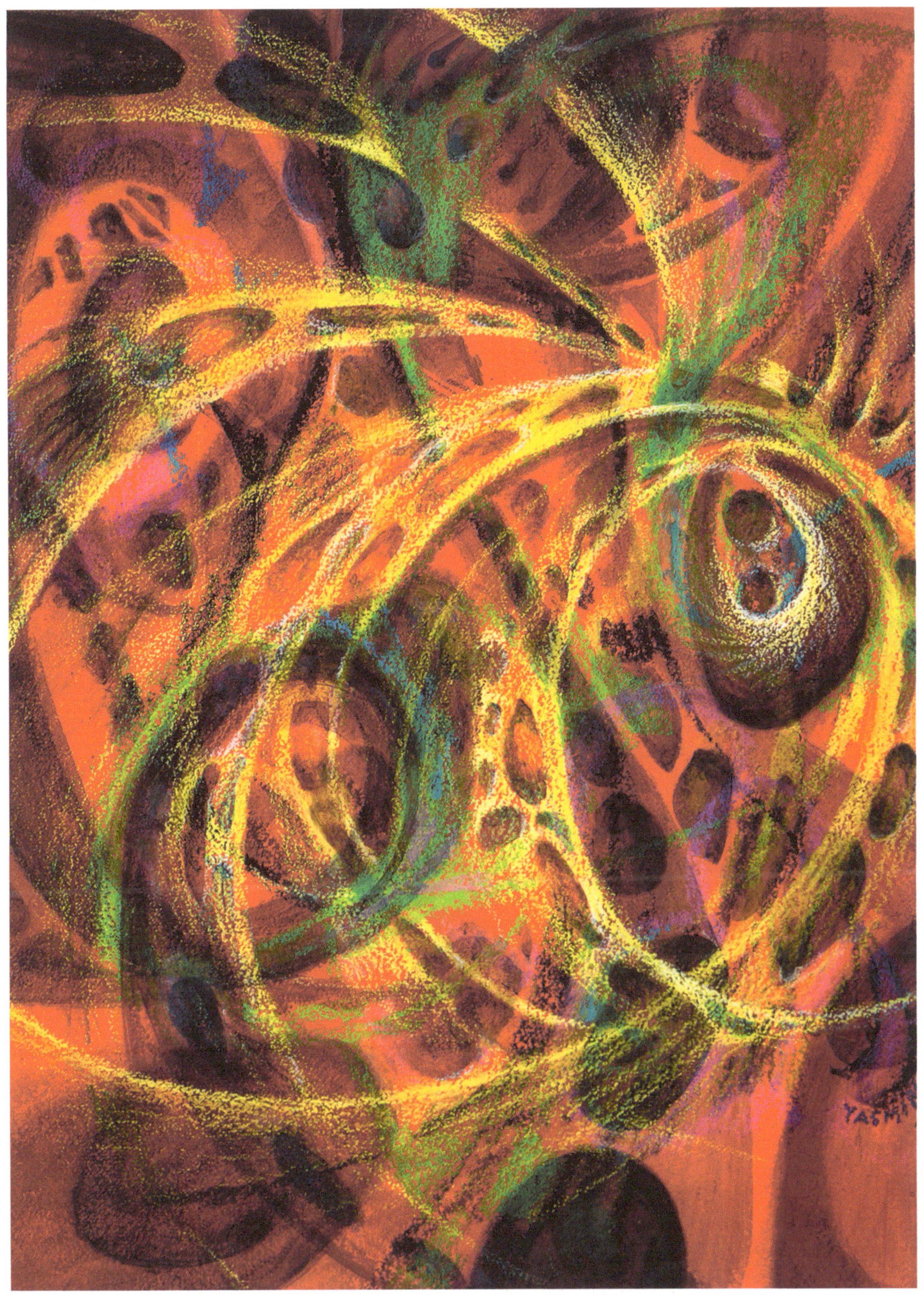

PLATE 9

Honoring the Ancestors

We climb the backs of our ancestors
and stand on their shoulders
to see the world as we do
May they be pleased
as we return to their arms

acrylic and oil pastels
30 x 22 inches

Page 30

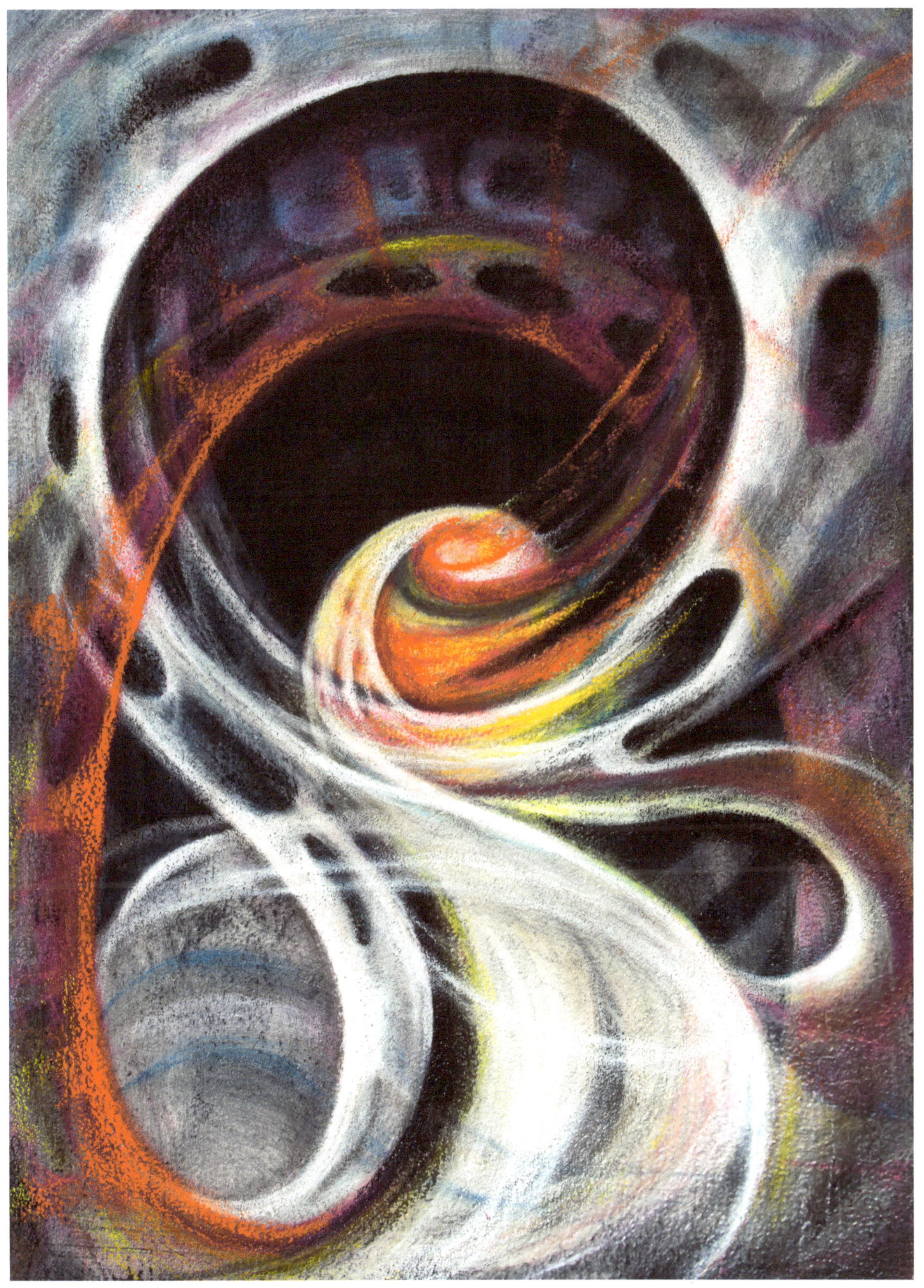

PLATE 10

Fusion

The union of being
melds
in the presence of creativity

acrylic and oil pastels
30 x 22 inches
collection of Penny Shrawder

Page 32

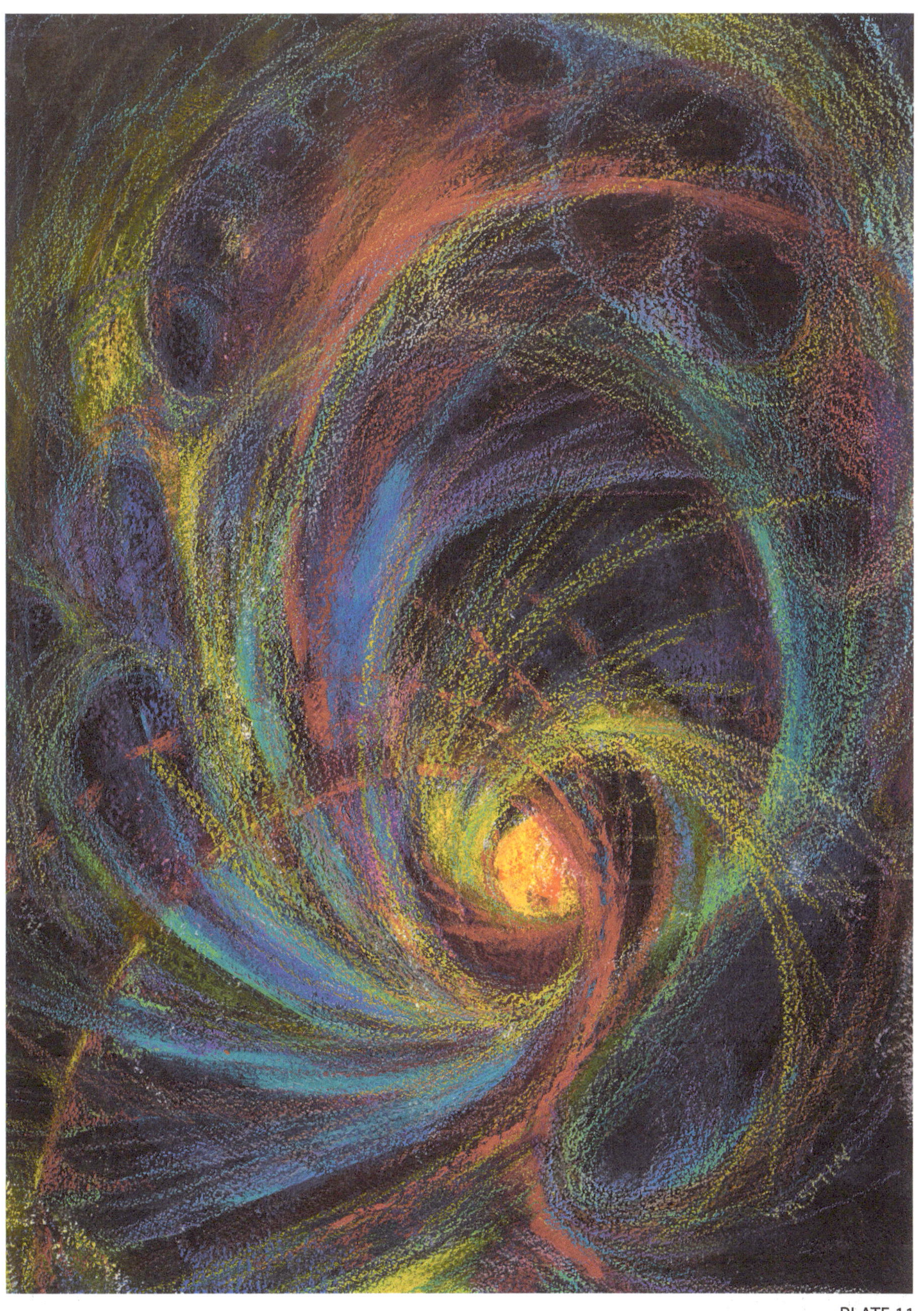

PLATE 11

Seeing at the Hem of Her Skirt

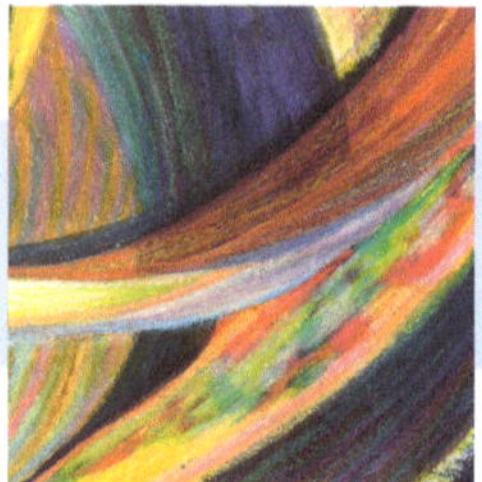

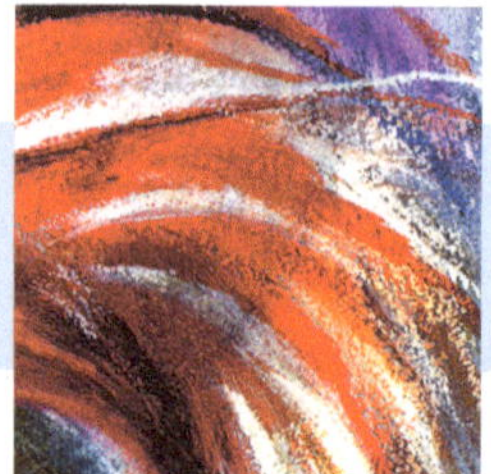

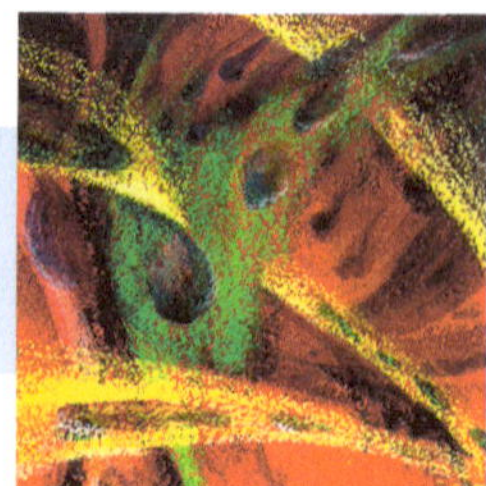

My grandmother lent me her skirt, at the hem of which I learned so much about life. With my pens and paintbrushes, I poet her impressions of the world. When my barely five-foot, squat Jamaican grandmother would can food, the smell was so sweet in my nose that its fragrance clung to my nostril hairs like fruit juice residue to my cup. I would sit on the floor not far from the stove in the kitchen of our New York home and absorb the sensory delights.

As a youngster, I often spent many hours tagging behind her holding on to the hem of her skirt and loving the extra attention she managed always to give to me. She'd tell me about many things … what spices danced together to delight, what herbs cured what illnesses, how to wash both house and body, and how in general to be in the world. She would tell me many things and then caution … but *behavior bespeaks beliefs.*

This is the way to set the dinner table, the only way to present yourself publicly, the only way to sit and still be viewed as a lady. Sometimes the list seemed inexhaustible: Wash your hands after using the commode, and before preparing or eating food. Walk like a lady, sit like one too.... Don't smack your lips while chewing food; don't talk with food in your mouth. Remember food gets passed from the right to the left; you hearing me, Girlie?

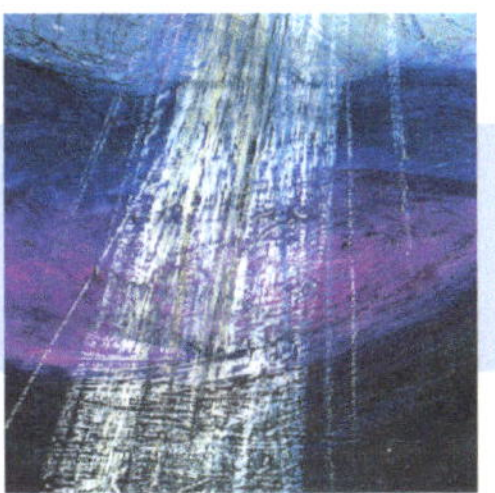
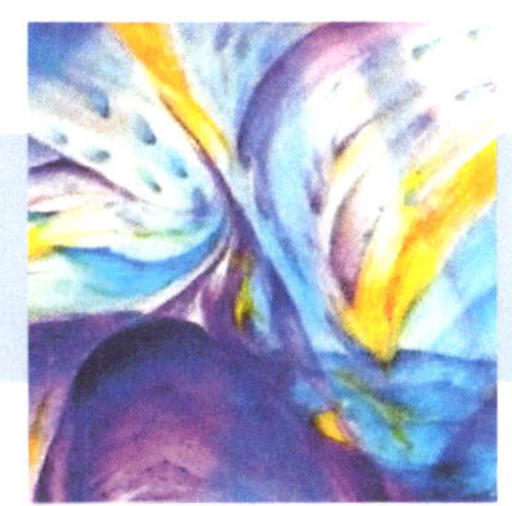
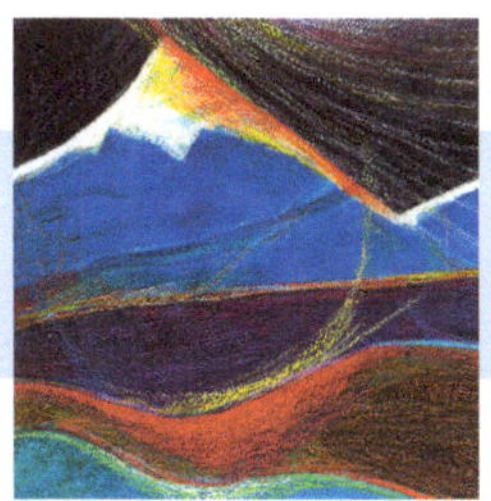

Don't leave home unless you have washed your body, tended to your toiletries and checked the long mirror. You belong to a people, and to a family name. This is how long your skirt should be and not a fraction shorter. Don't be or associate with hussies. Remember, If you lie down with dogs you will get up with fleas. Don't sass your elders. Never bow before anyone, but God. Are you listening to me? Never leave hair in your comb or brush; burn it! One strand of hair and folks can know all there is to know about you. Don't let a boy hold your hand, because holding your hand is never enough to satisfy what he really wants. Keep your panties up and your dress down; your virtue is your honor. Always remember to respect yourself then others will have no valid reason to disrespect you. Remember, wishes won't wash the dishes, and if you plant the seeds of tomatoes you will not harvest carrots. Hold your head up; keep your shoulders unhunched and your back erect. Remember, You choose whether you have a wishbone or a backbone. When life gets hard, and it will, brace that backbone that you've inherited from generation after generation of African women.... Don't go to an olive tree looking for figs. Get your dead in the ground fast. Don't eat behind nasty people. Unplug all electrical things when there is a lightning storm. Put a patty of grated, brown soap and sugar on a boil if you want to draw the infection. Don't get to thinking you're grown just because you are old enough to start smelling yourself. Hold gratitude in your heart always. Remember to call the names and feed the spirits of the ancestors, for they are the bosoms that offer us comfort in the trials and tribulations of life. Stand tall, make your kinfolks proud, and remember how I raised you up. At the hem of her skirt, I learned to see the world, and many of my mannerisms I imprinted from her lips to my heart.

Behavior Bespeaks Beliefs

Let the words of my mouth
meet the intentions
of my deeds
and there amplify and exalt

acrylic and oil pastels
30 x 22 inches

Page 36

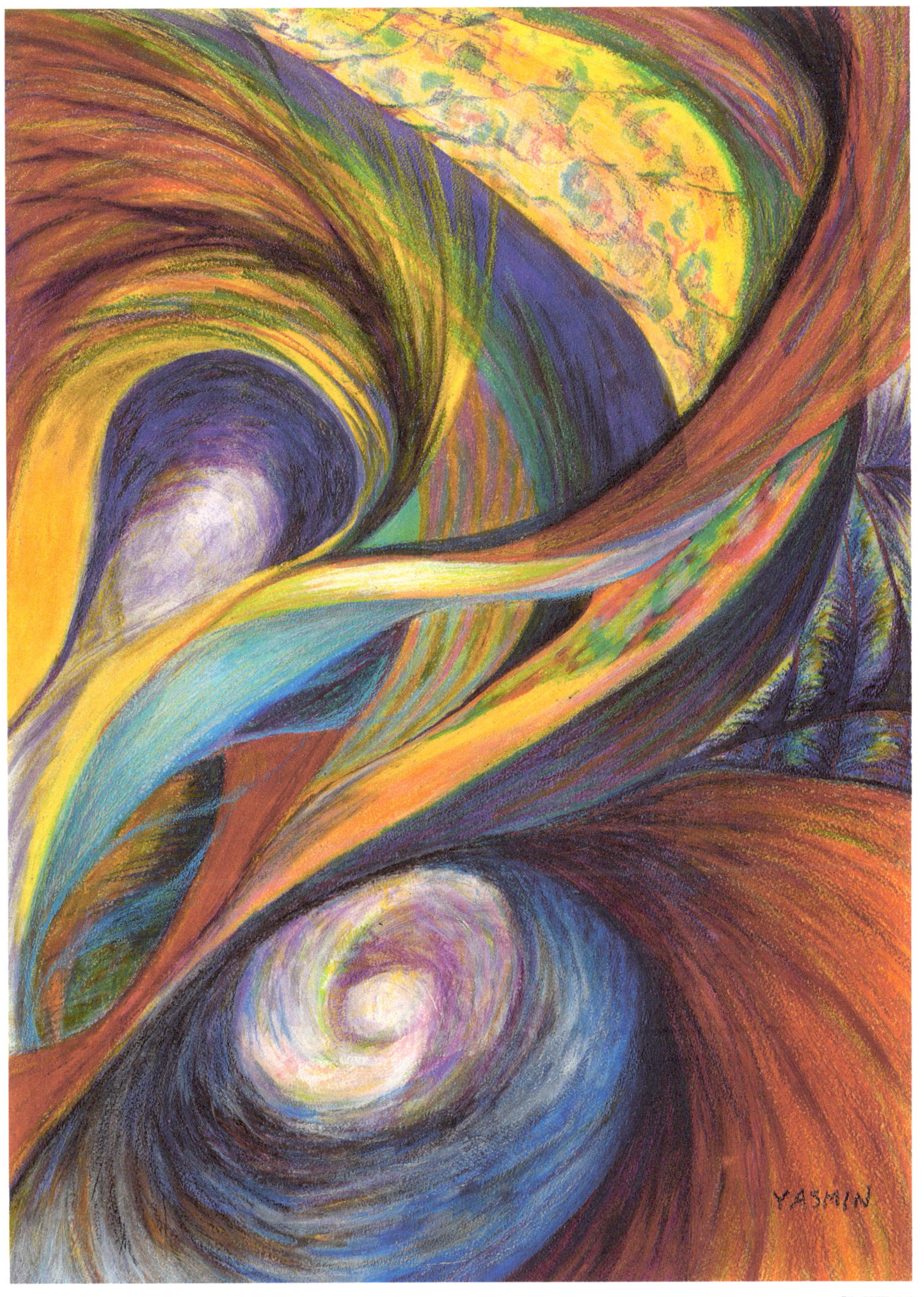

PLATE 12

Most High: Forever Loving Thee

Inviolable space
Where no one and
nothing alters or dismisses
connections between
Thee and me

acrylic and oil pastels
30 x 22 inches
collection of Zenny Groce

Page 38

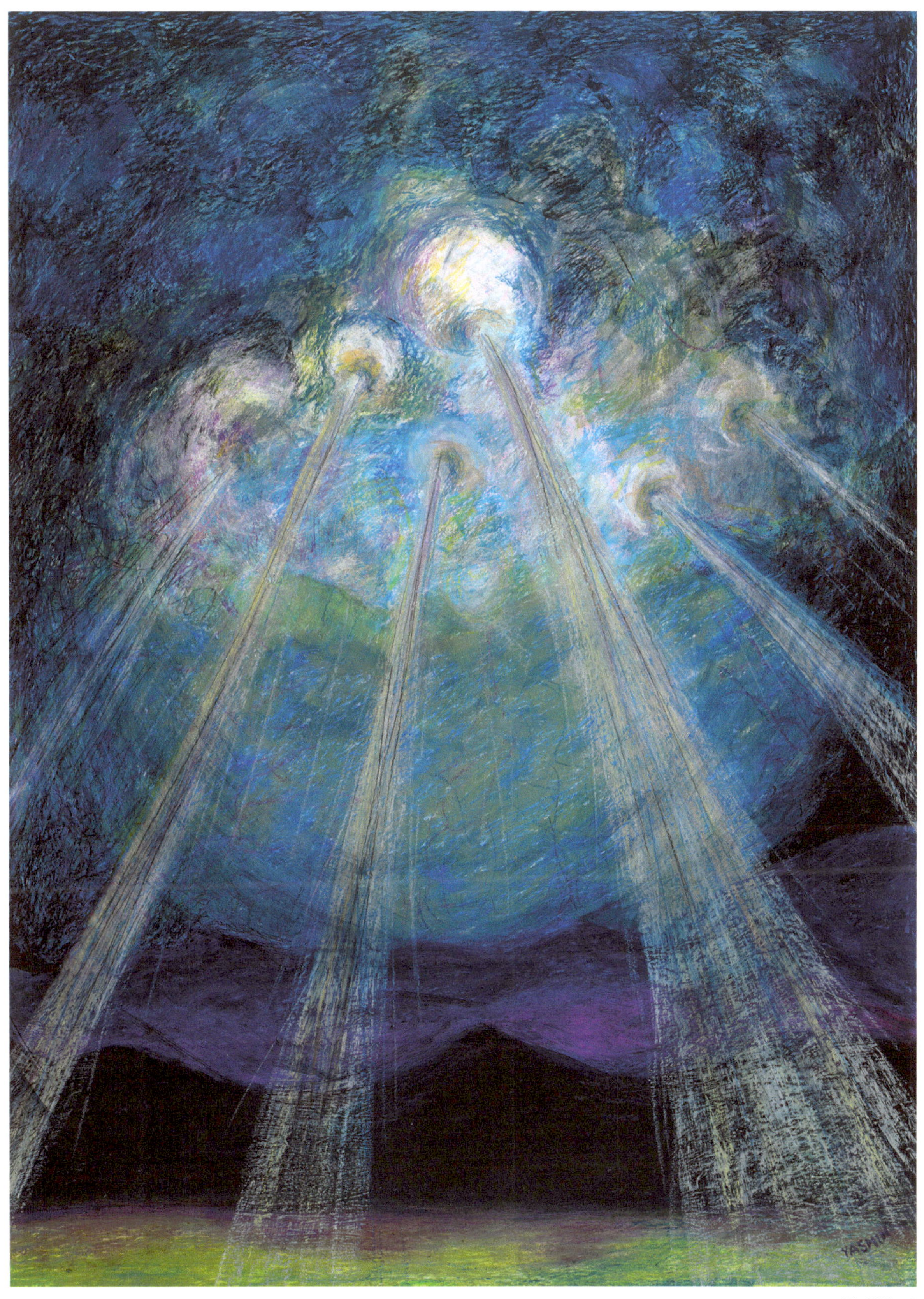

PLATE 13

Peace Be Still

May peace be still in the hearts of humanity
Where tempests rage
and polarities stake
may middle ways
be forged

acrylic and oil pastels
60 x 48 inches

Page 40

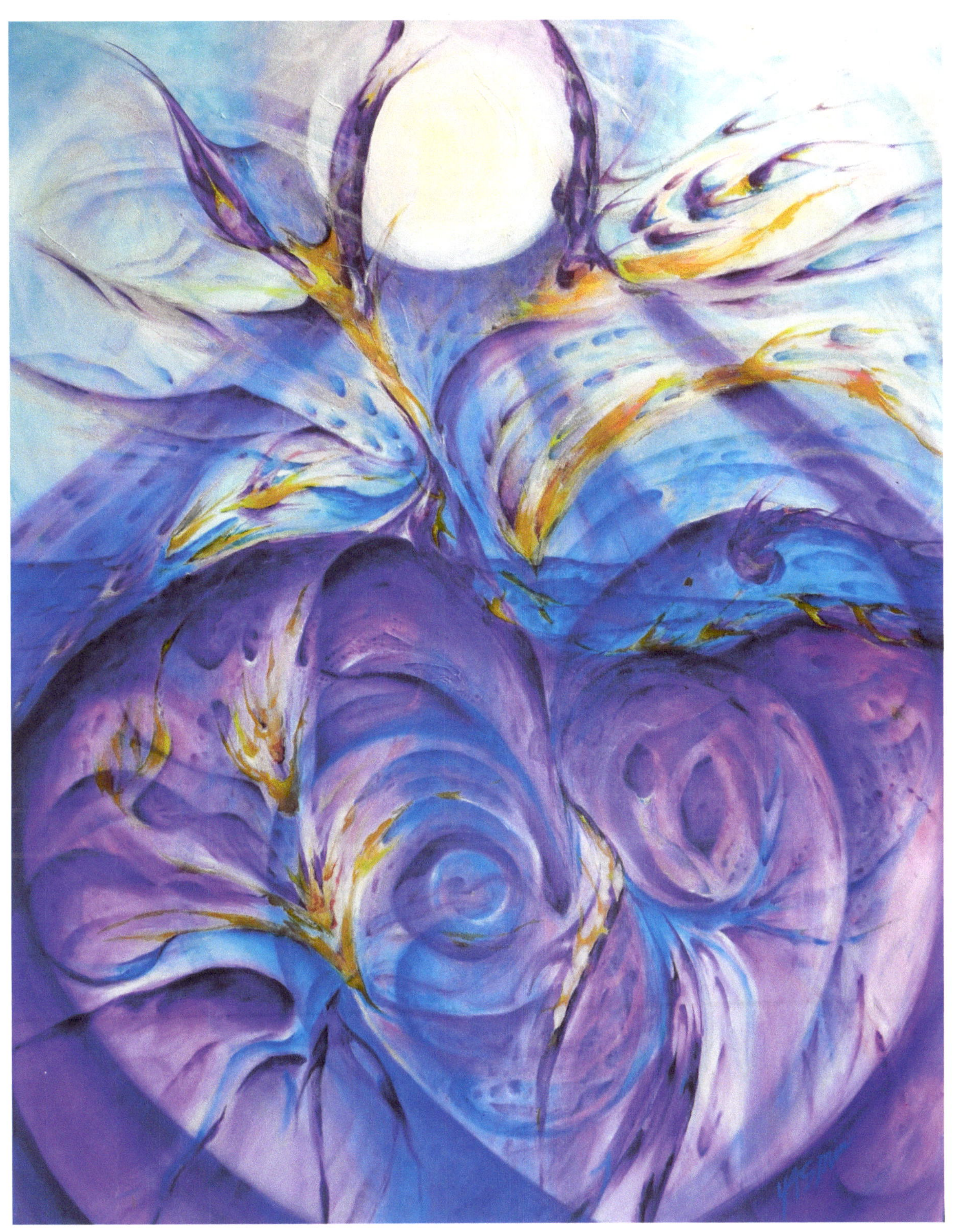

PLATE 14

Bowing in Deference

Behold the sacred
In deference bow
Character walk
Peace pray
and justice work

acrylic and oil pastels
30 x 22 inches
collection of Theresa Souers

Page 42

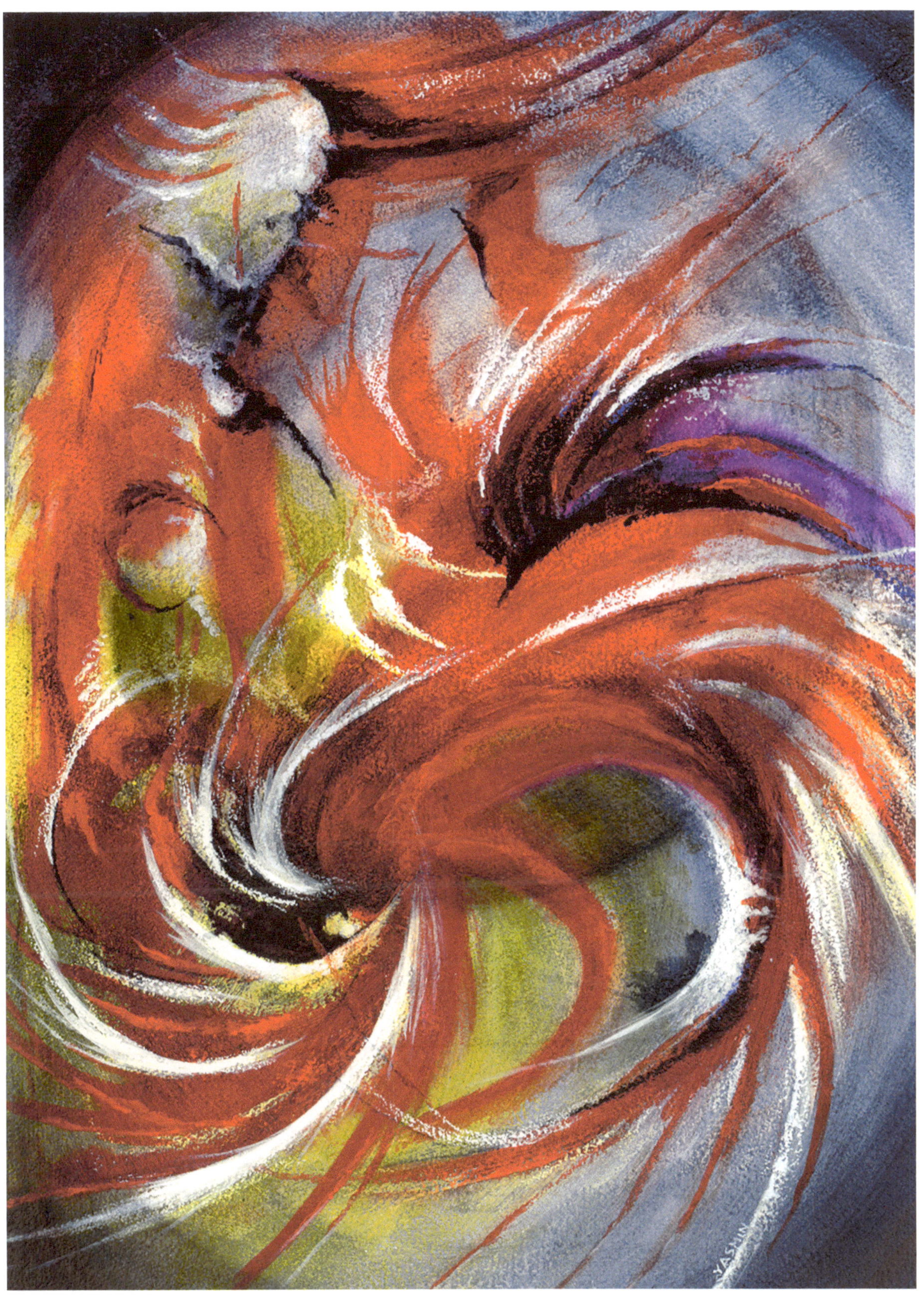

PLATE 15

Dancing with Divinity

Magnificence and elegance …
Word weaving
Spinning intoxicating joy
beyond the confines
of word

acrylic and oil pastels
30 x 22 inches

Page 44

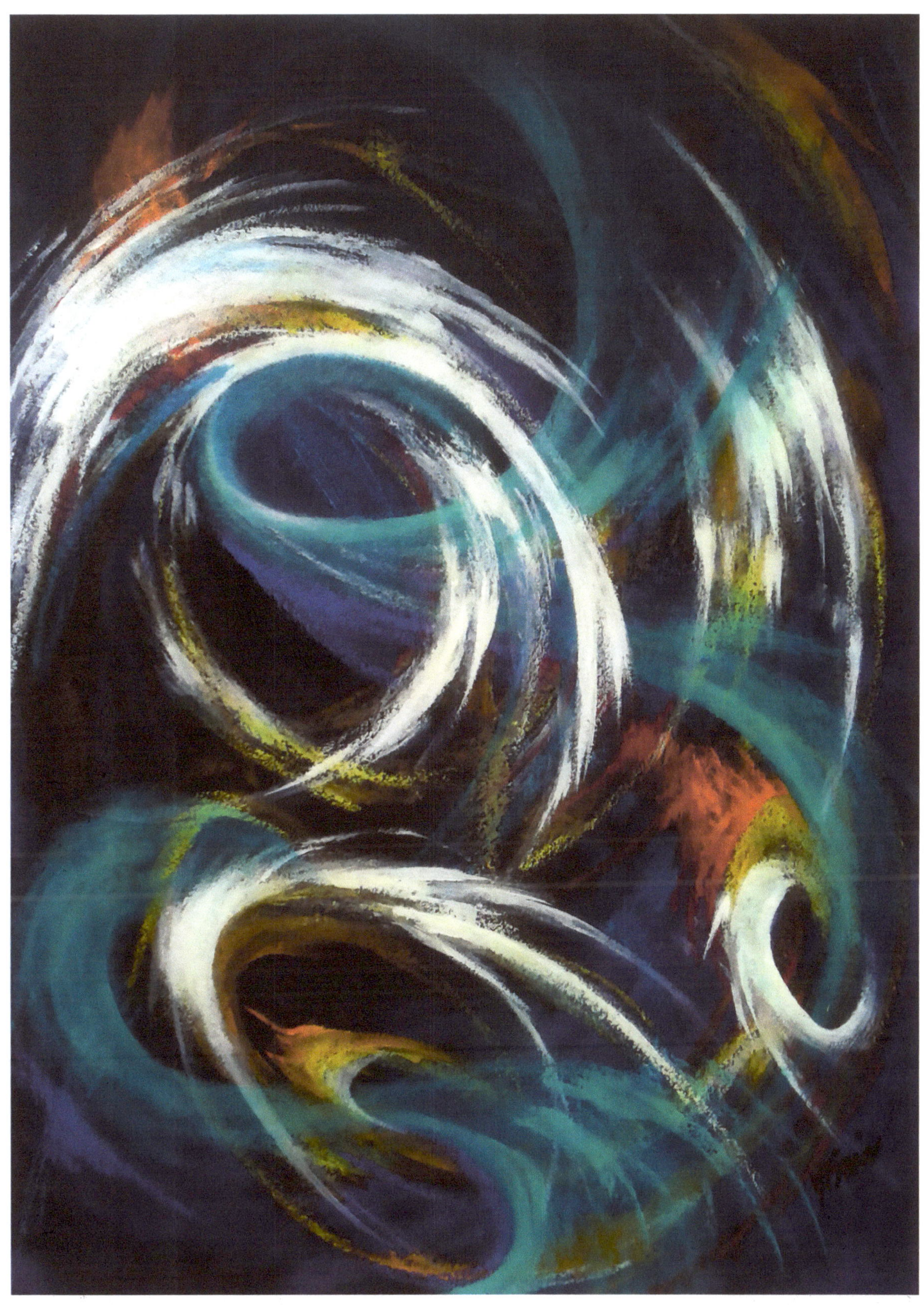

PLATE 16

Majesty

Every sunrise
and set
a new beginning
and closing of opportunities

Landscapes explored and revisited
expressing majesty
and magnificence
in the presence of nature's wonders

acrylic and oil pastels
30 x 22 inches
collection of Douglas W. Renk

Page 46

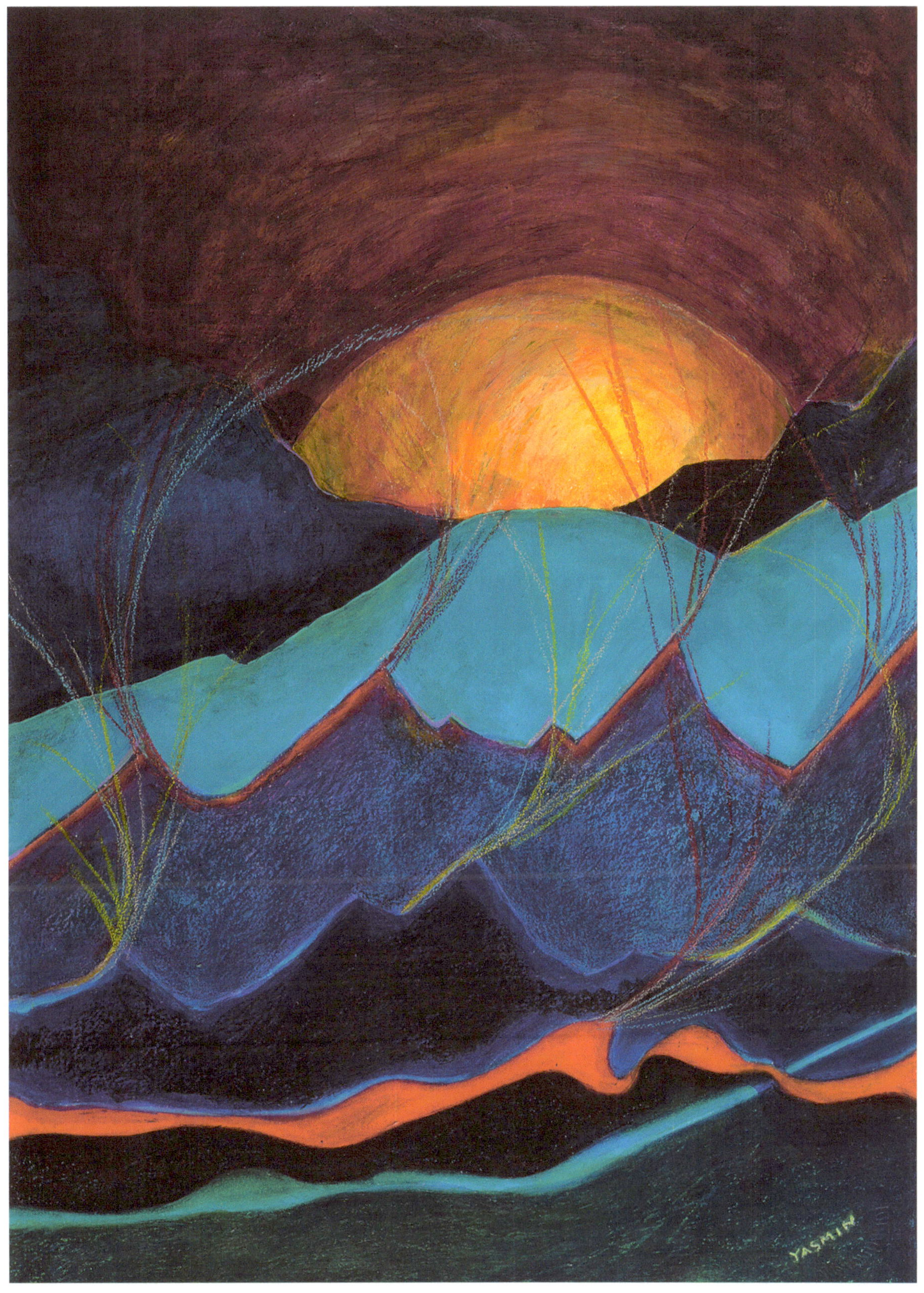

PLATE 17

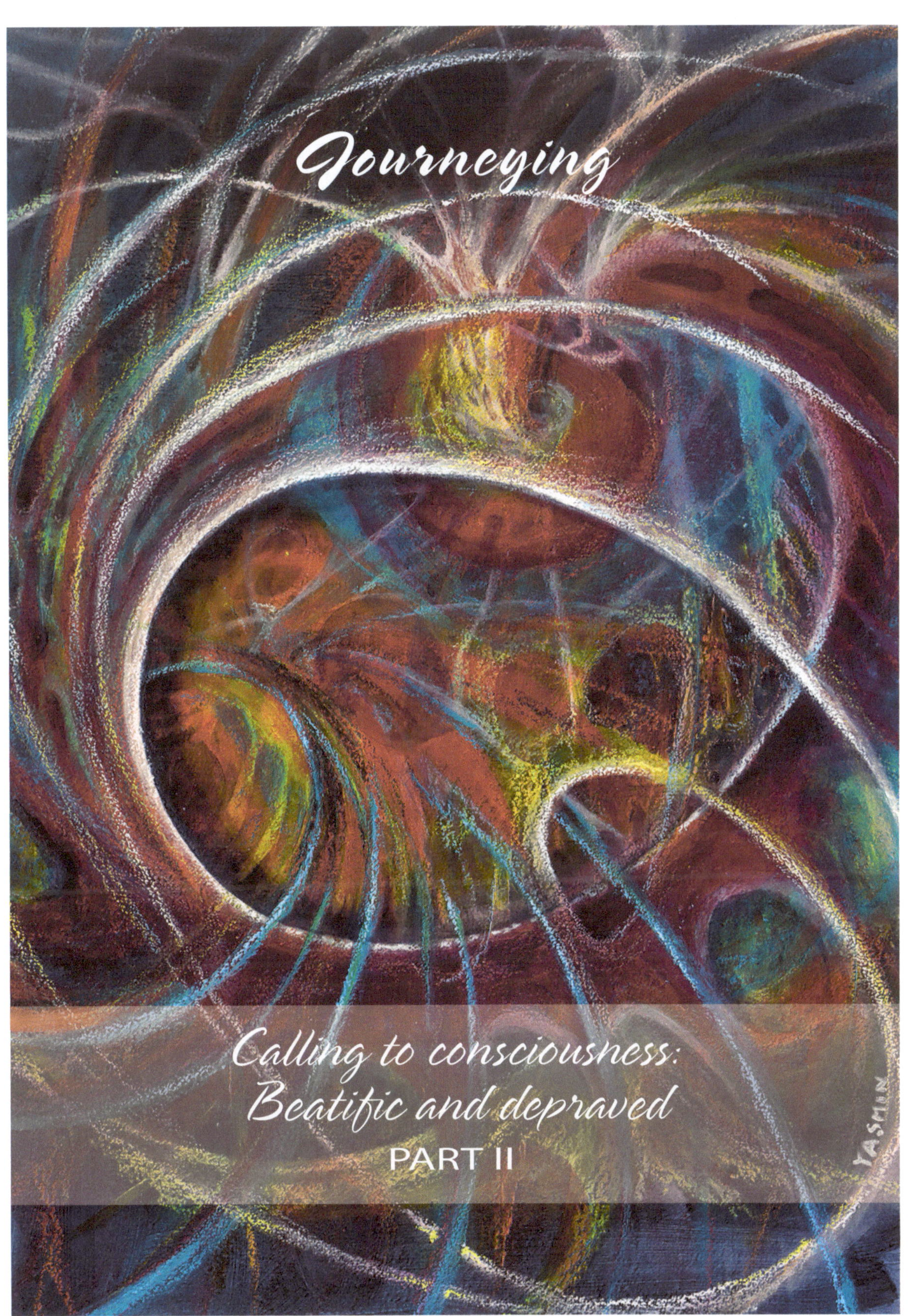
Journeying
Calling to consciousness:
Beatific and depraved
PART II
YASMIN

Journeying: Limitations as Opportunities

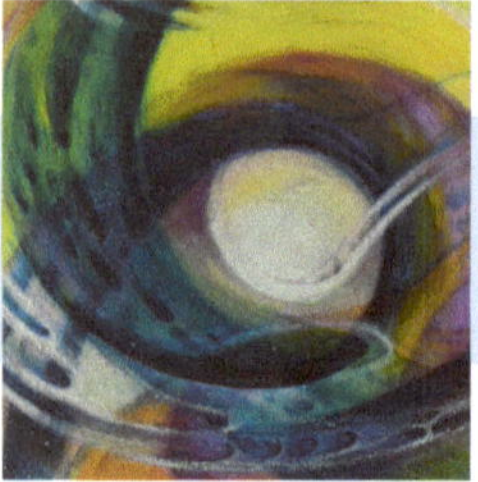 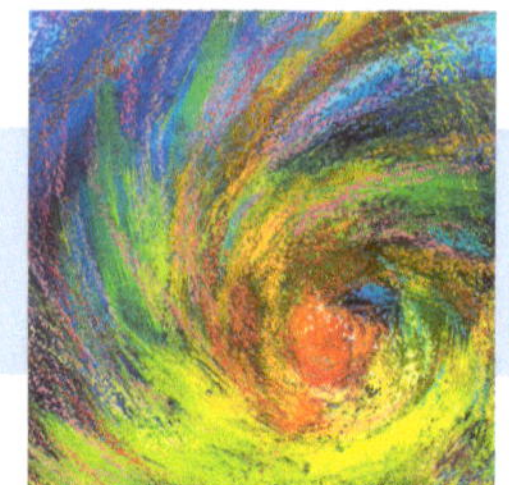 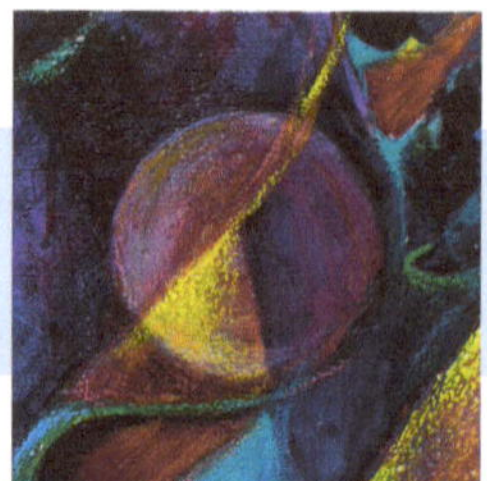

When lions have historians then hunters will cease to be heroes —South African saying

One day when there was much commotion in my home, neighbors had gathered to watch a colored man play baseball. I ran outside hoping the iridescent glittering puddle was still available and wondered if this colored man would look at all like that of its reflections. I wondered just how magnificent this colored man must look. With anticipatory delight, I rejoined the community, eating treats and staring at the black and white television, waiting to see the potential richness of the special man's color.

I was a budding artist of five or six years old. I mixed poster paint for my pictures and designs. I liked bright colors, again wondering the colored man's hue. My mind raced: would he be patterned like the veins of a leaf made translucent by holding it towards the light, or textured like the sand dampened by water droplets? Would he be rainbow colored or intricate like the circular stained glass window in the attic? What make and manner must be this man? I shared the breadth of my imagination with no one. I wanted to see if my inside image matched the television image of the man from Brooklyn. I had an auntie who lived in Brooklyn whom we sometimes drove to visit, but I couldn't remember ever seeing a colored man there. I couldn't remember ever seeing a colored woman or child either. I was thusly excited about seeing the Brooklyn-Dodger-colored-man.

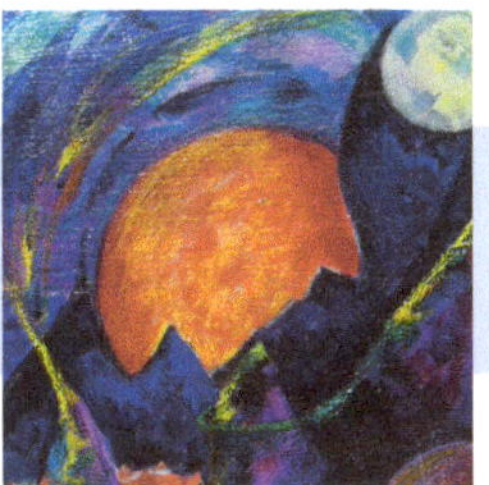
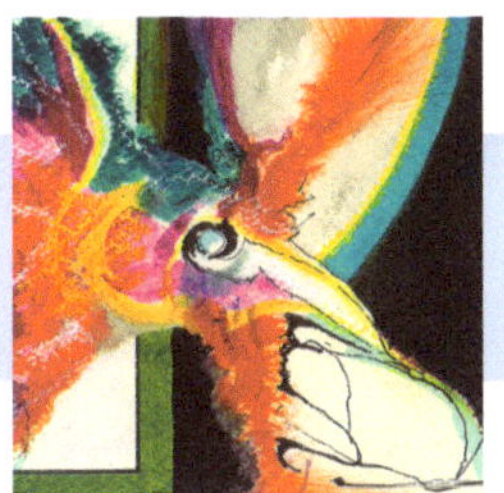
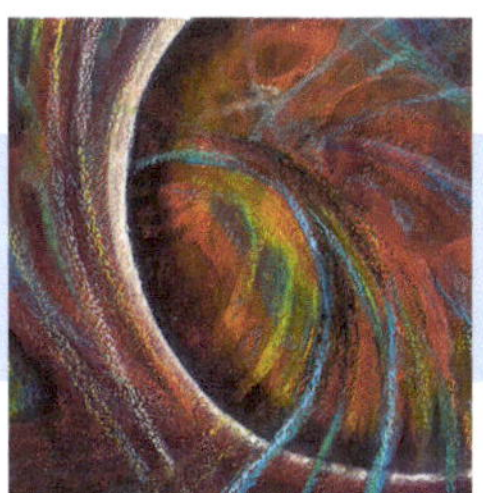

As he stepped to the baseball plate, cheers filled the room. My heart sunk in utter dismay; he was no more, no less distinguished than the men who cheered. I wondered what was so special about this man? A neighbor, just back from some military campaign said after I queried their excitement, that it was such a big deal for Jackie Robinson, a colored man, to play in the National Baseball League. "Why," I asked. "Because America doesn't like colored people and Mr. Robinson is breaking the color line that separates us from other Americans". "Us?" Were they colored, was I, did America not like me? I did not know until that day that I was colored, different, and despised.

I stared at my hands and watched a trust I had in the world, and my place in it become altered. A sense of my specialness sloughed from consciousness. I belonged to a despised group. Colored slowly tinted and colored slowly refracted the lens through which I perceived the world and myself therein. Some piece of innocence faded into the background of coloredness. I had inconsolable grief and went to lie in the grass, to hold hands towards the sky, where I stared until I slipped into the veins, traveled the forms, and wanted hands borrowed from *Spirit* to bring messages of peace and fairness.

Limitations as Opportunities

The sweetnesses
of salt
await
but our
recognition

acrylic and oil pastels
30 x 22 inches
collection by Robert Fong

Page 52

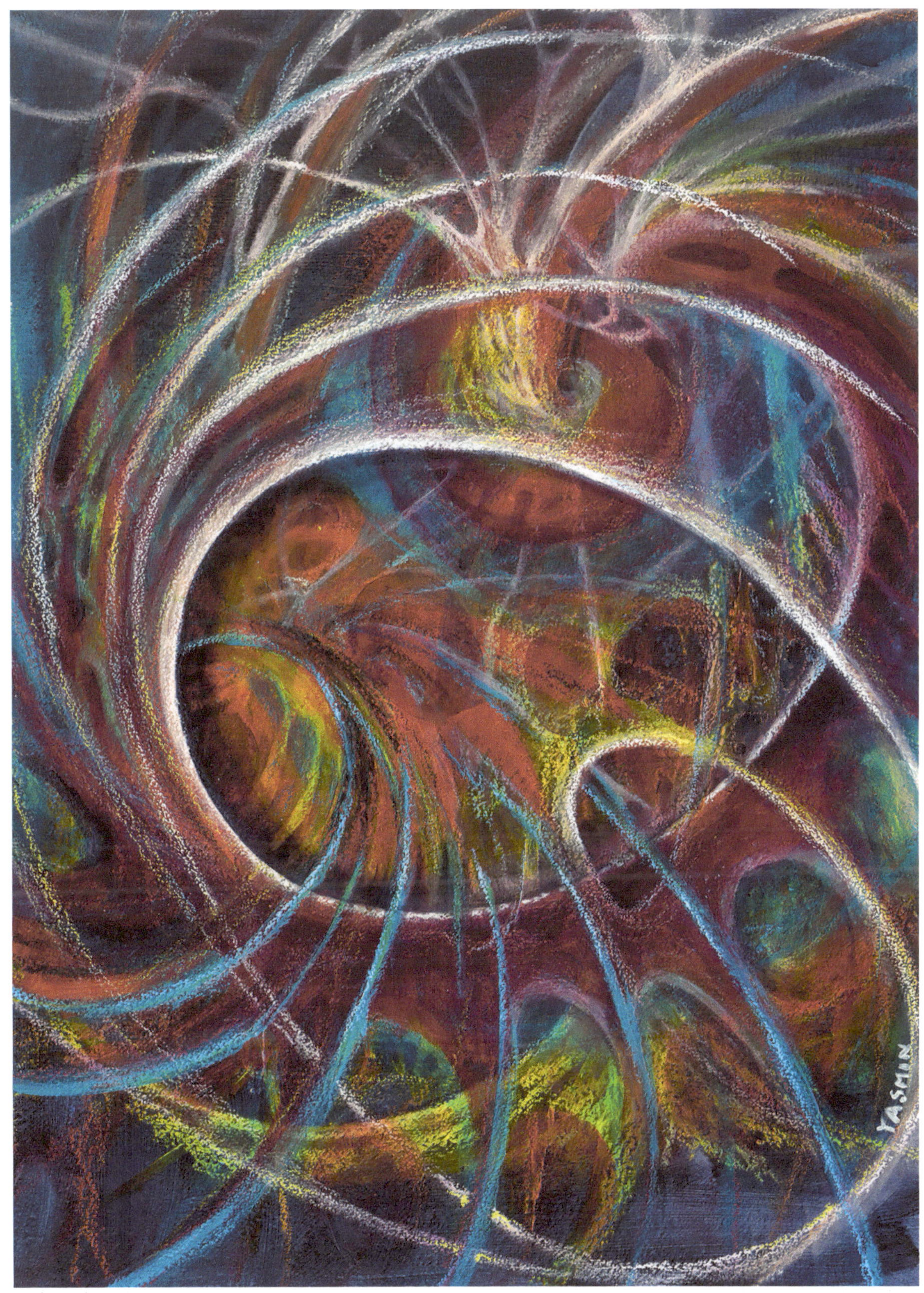

PLATE 18

Watch Night Bird: Looking out for freedom

Anticipatory
watching
whispers
hopes and
dreams anew
Emancipation!

watercolor ink
24 x 18 inches
collection of Leah Rescate

Page 54

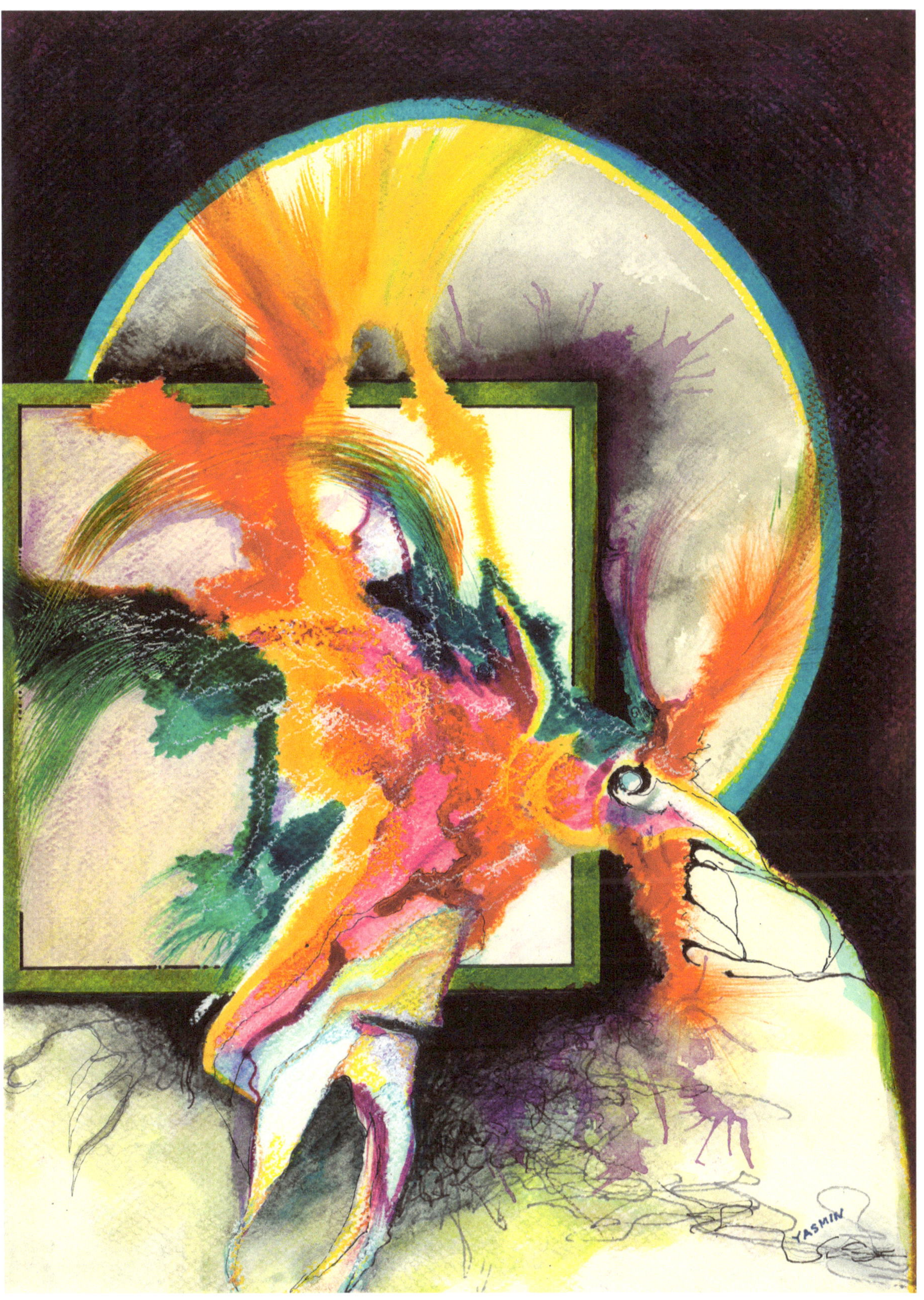

PLATE 19

Awakening

In moments of awareness
commodious choices present

watercolor ink and acrylic
18 x 24 inches
collection of Nancy Stuart

Page 56

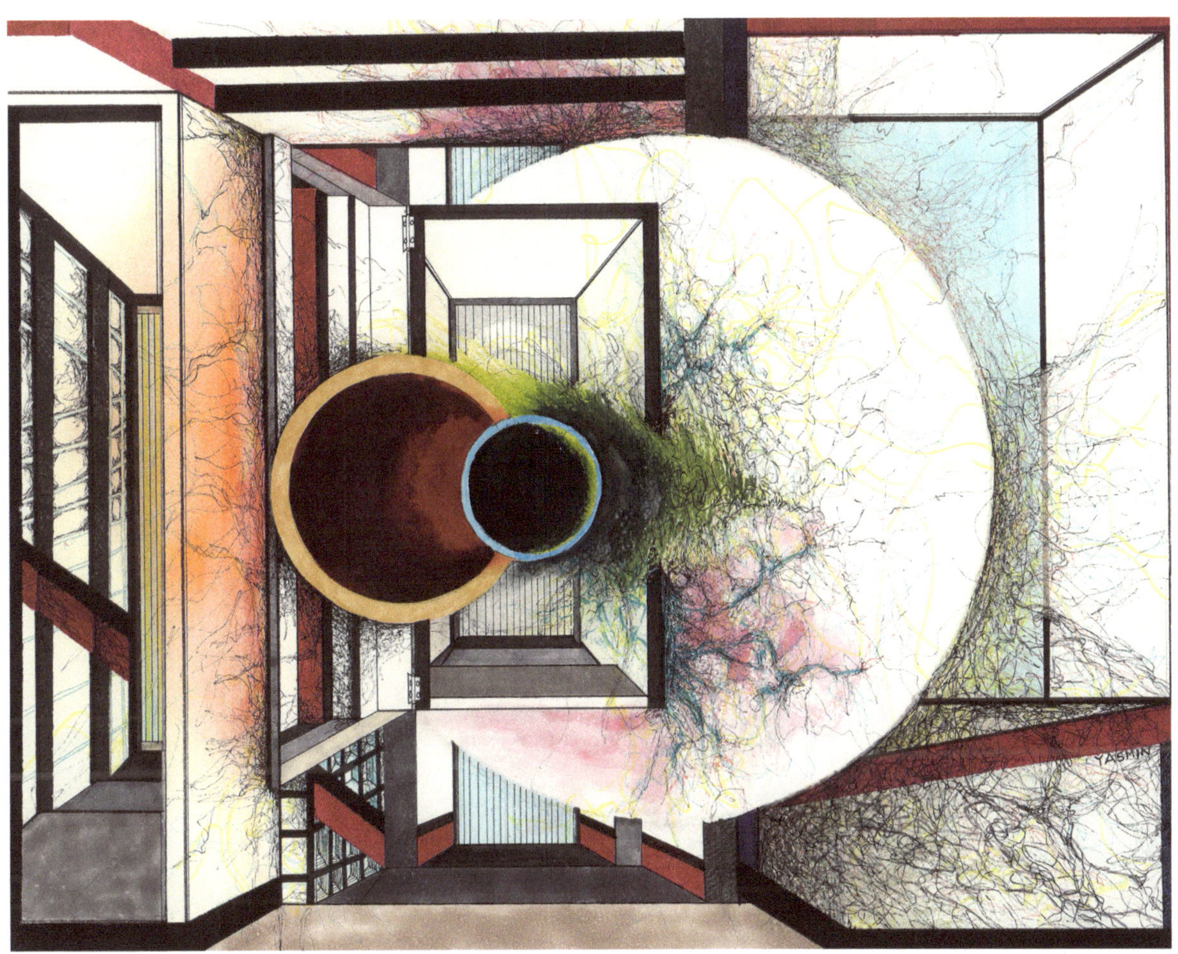

PLATE 20

Awakening II

Conscious blooms
awaiting
our footprints

watercolor ink and acrylic
18 x 24 inches

Page 58

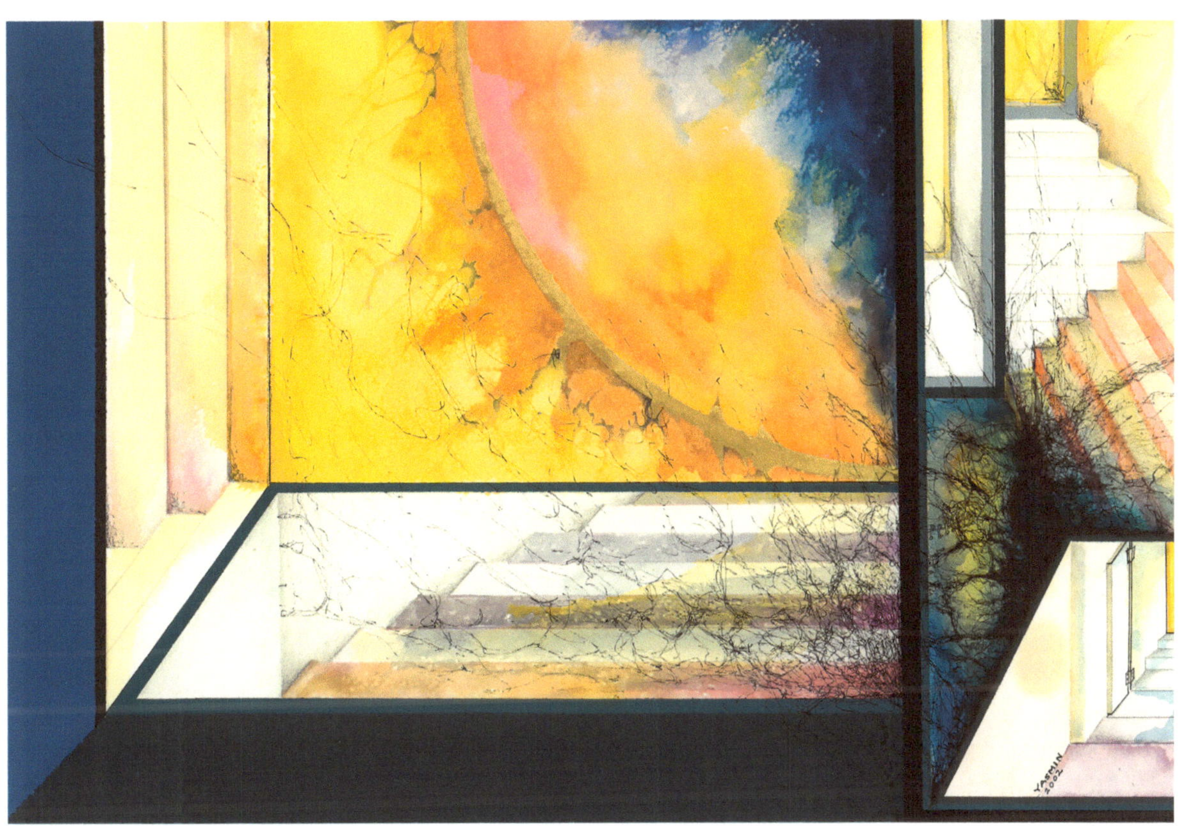

PLATE 21

Spirits Leaving (9/11 Series)

Life, fragile
Promises of tomorrow
nonexistent
Spirits making journeys home
unexpectedly

acrylic and oil pastels
22 x 30 inches

Page 60

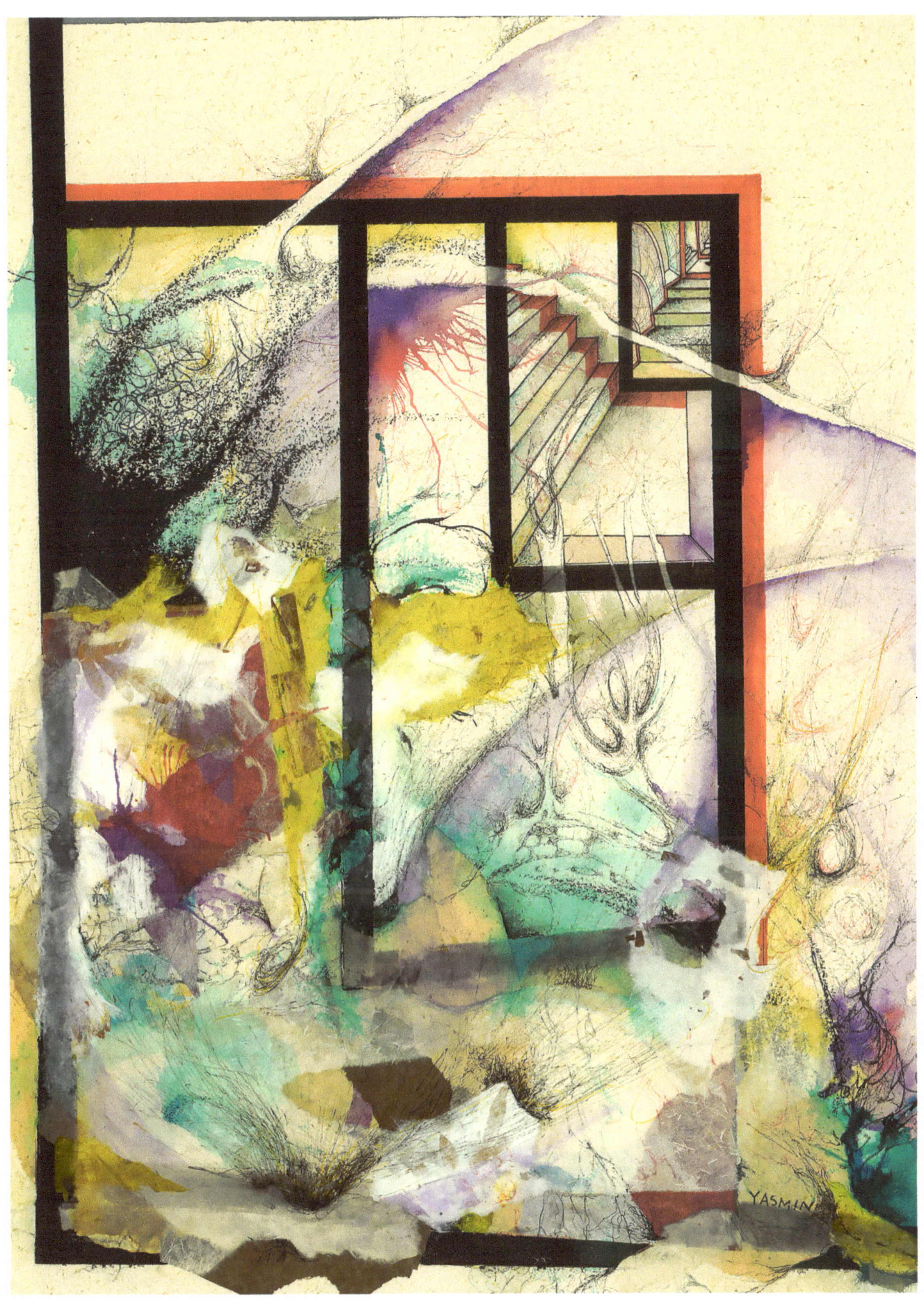

PLATE 22

9/11

Horrific the attacks
the aftermaths and
lives disrupted
Miracles, courage and nobility arose from the rumbles
Blessed the survival of my sister
Truth and reconciliation
model behavior elegant
and life-affirming
Hunting and murdering offenders
reaffirms neither truth, nor reconciliation of wrongdoings
Sad the decisions of revenge
Sad the choice of lessons lost

acrylic and oil pastels
22 x 30 inches

Page 62

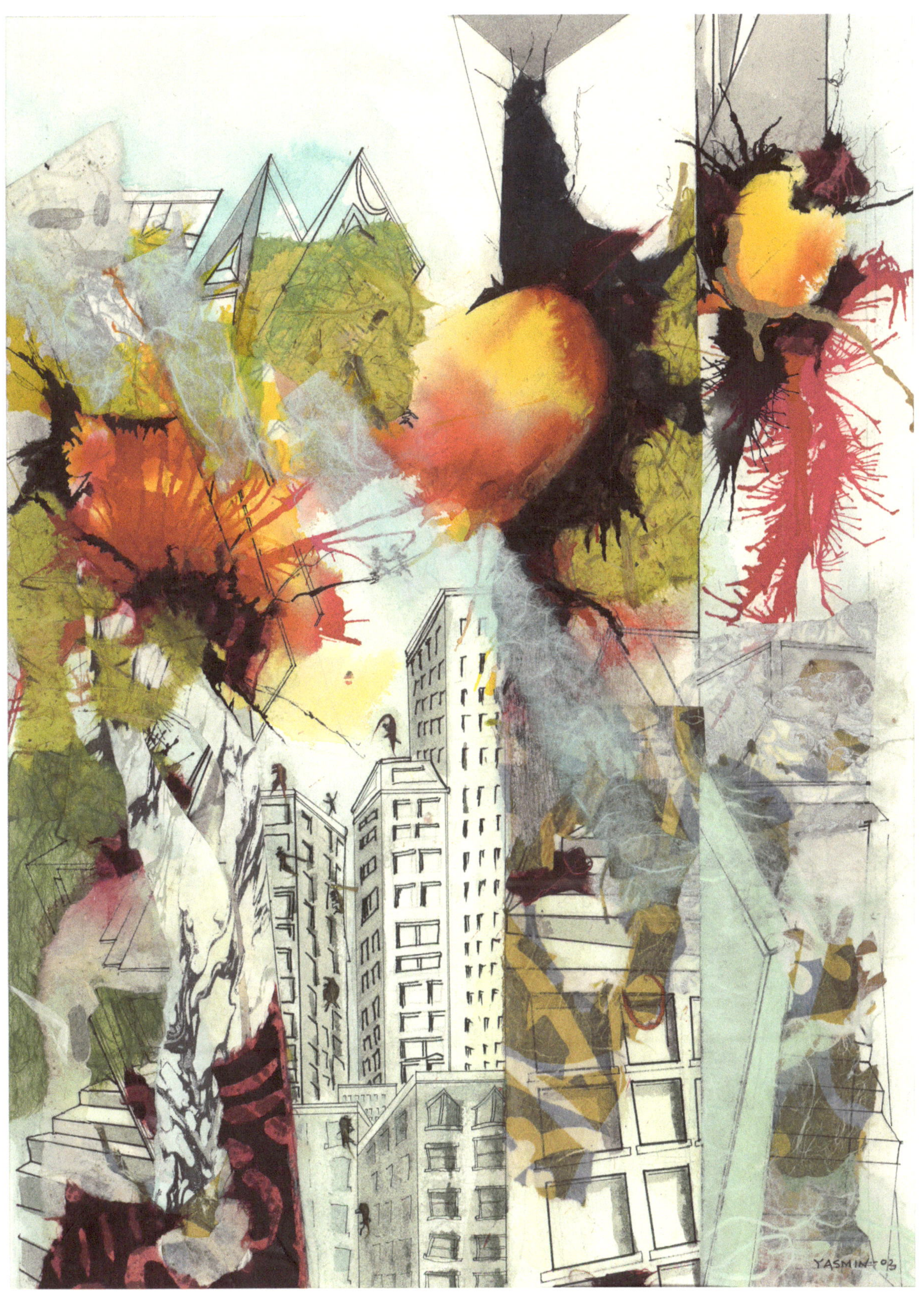

PLATE 23

Transformation

Variables meld
Shift
Substituting views
toward differing flows

acrylic and oil pastels
22 x 30 inches

Page 64

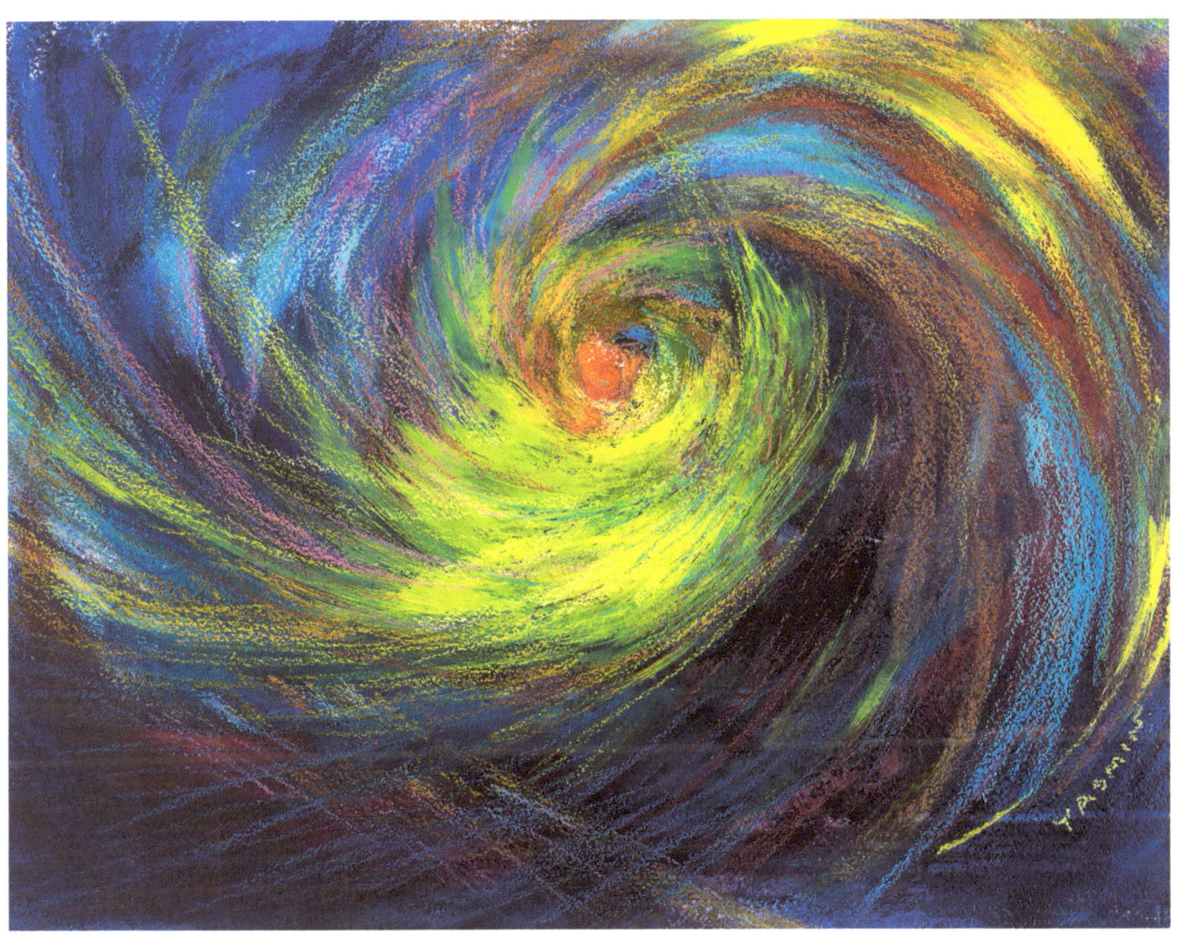

PLATE 24

Internal Landscape I

Internal reflects
External mirrors
looping continually
yonder and through
seeking
without end

acrylic and oil pastels
30 x 22 inches

Page 66

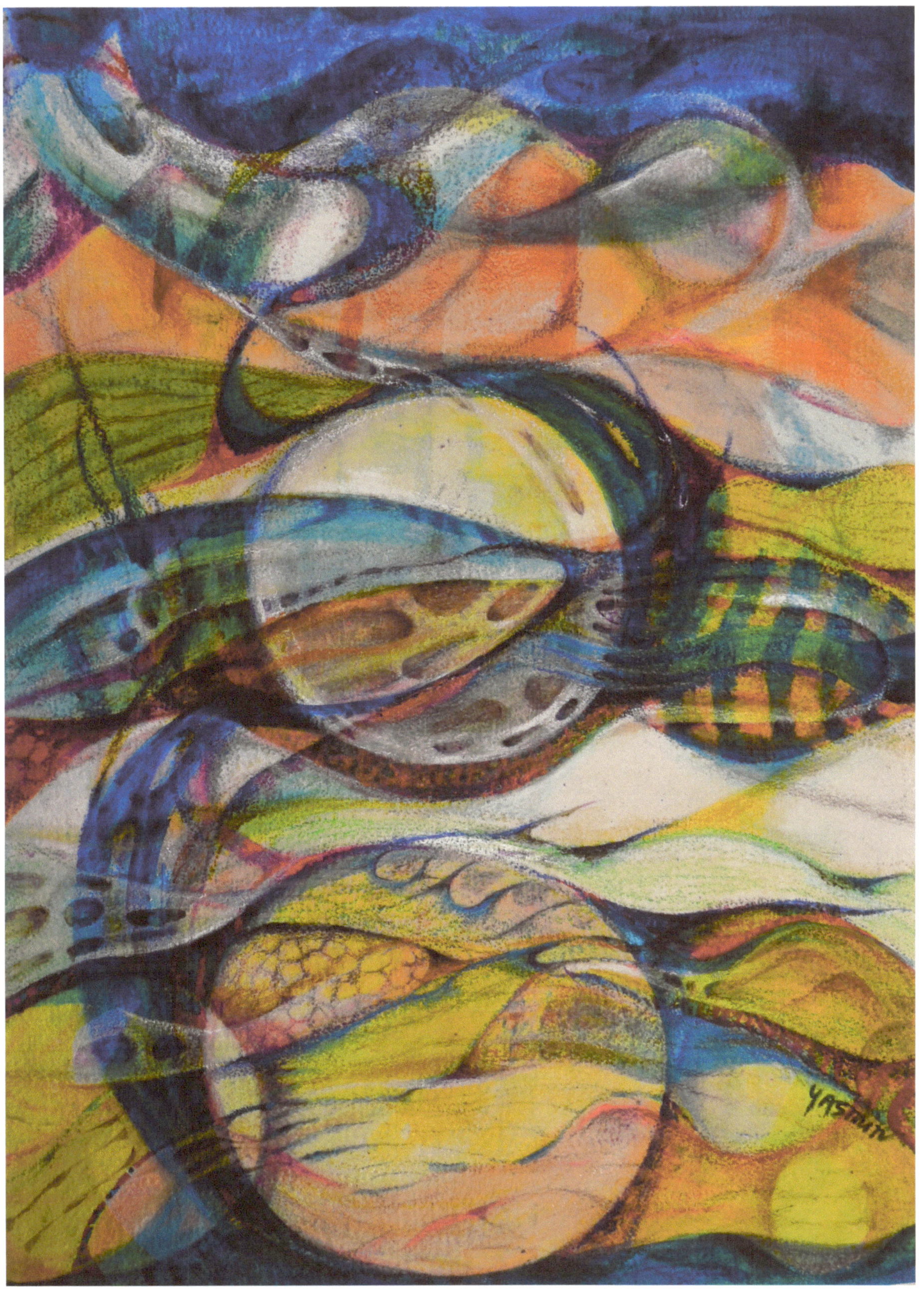

PLATE 25

Internal Landscape II

Rich are the gardens
illumined with paths
beckoned and chosen
Happiness and
tribulation alike
illumine and inform
knowingness

acrylic and oil pastels
30 x 22 inches

Page 68

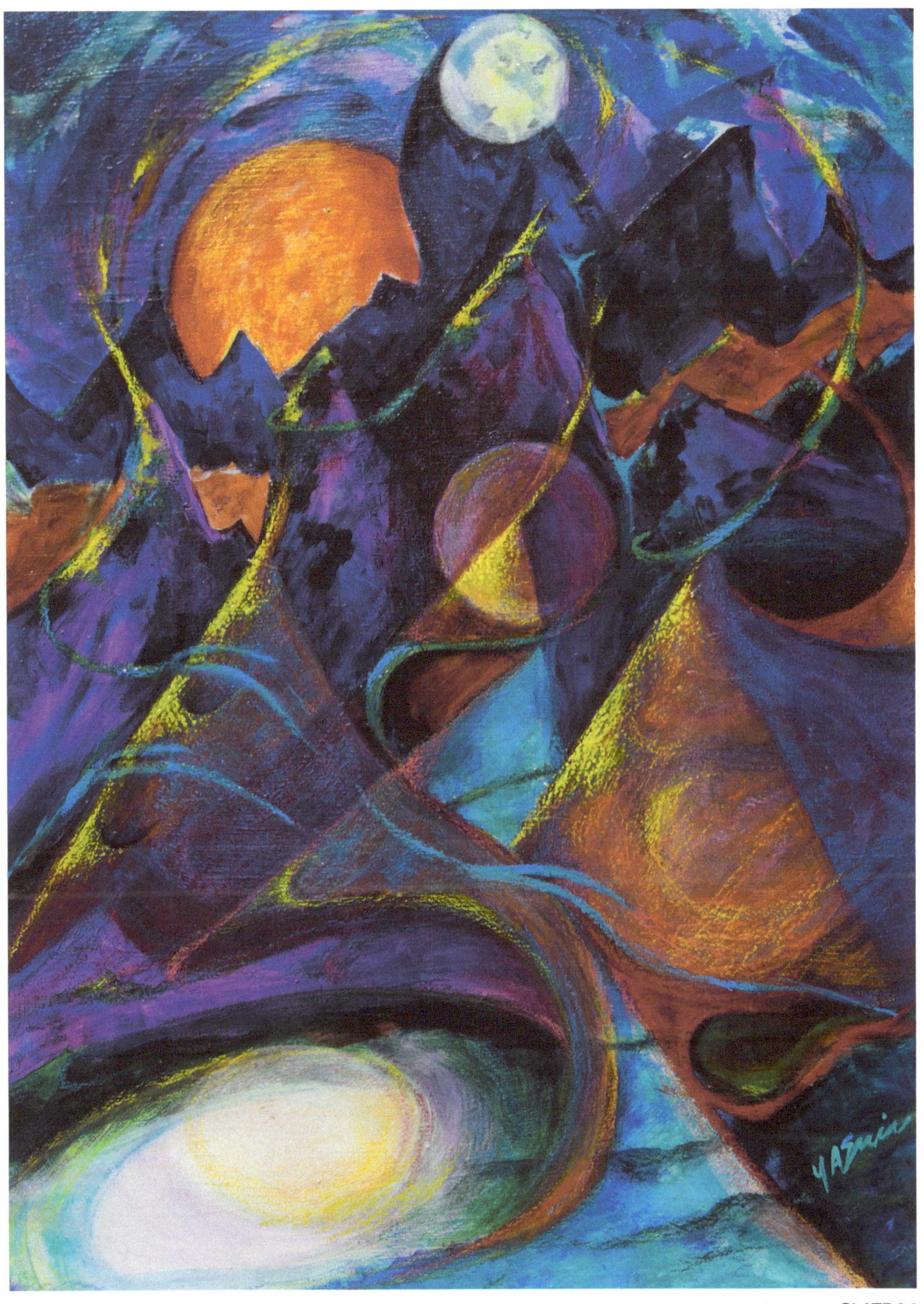

PLATE 26

The Inward journey

Wellsprings within which inspiration is cradled
Injuries soothed
Consciousness birthed
Thinkers formed

acrylic and oil pastels
30 x 22 inches

Page 70

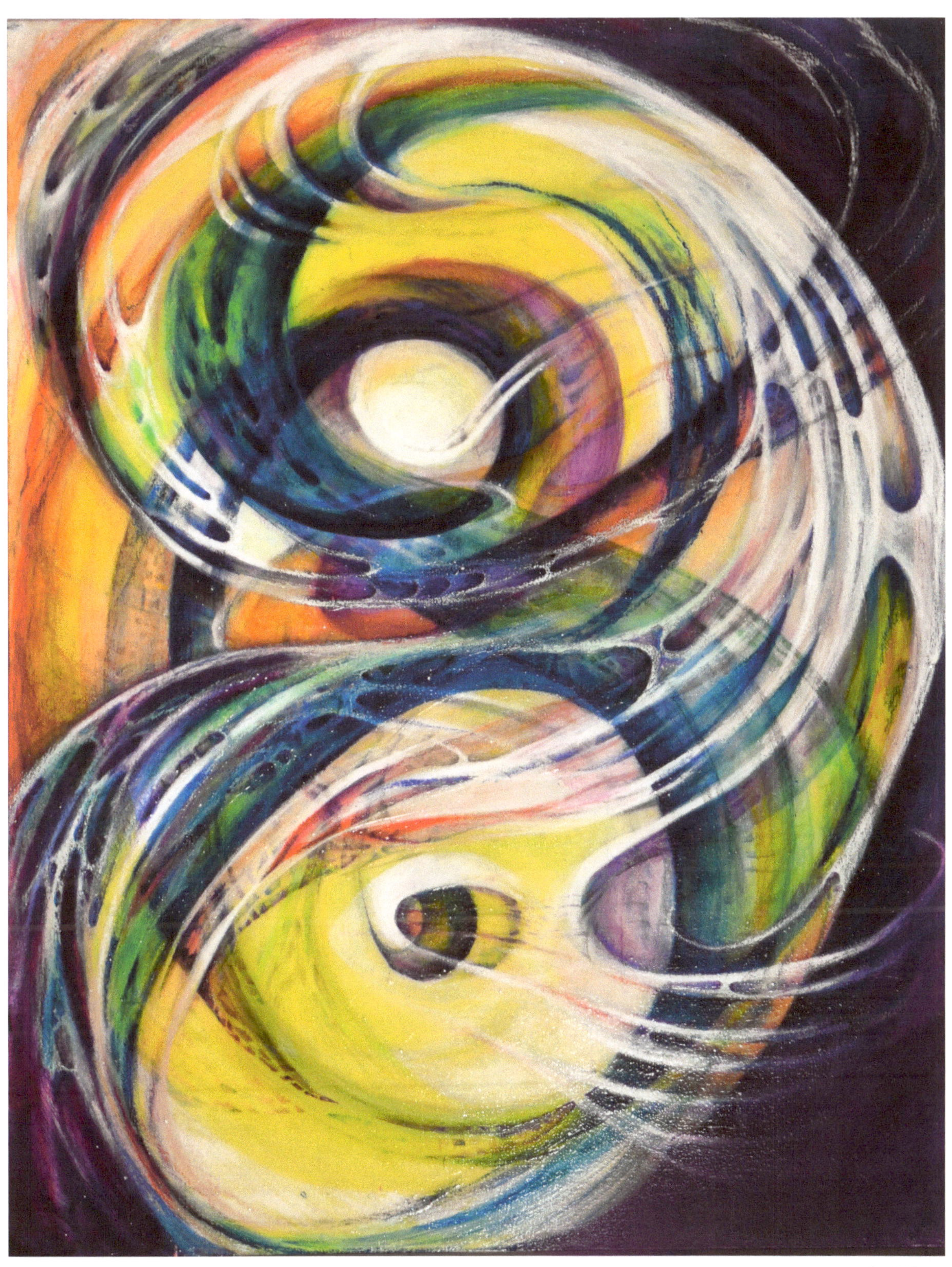

PLATE 27

Journeying: Beatific Flows of Life

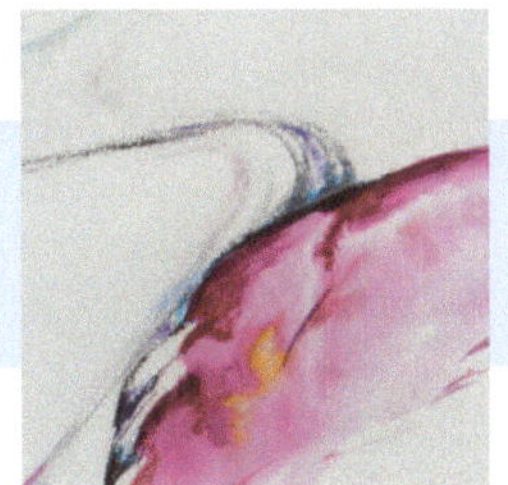

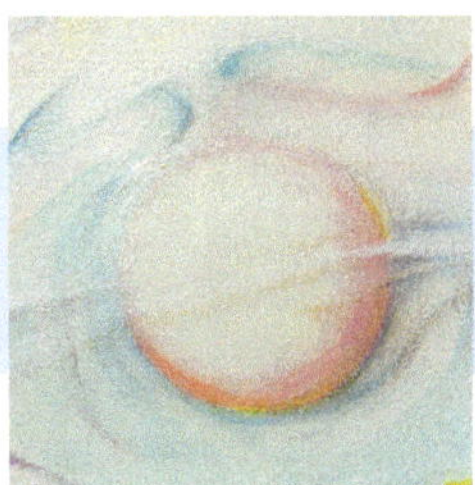

We live in a time that is simultaneously troublesome and promising, where the human spirit craves beauty, and definitions of altruism and compassion, and yearns for authentic connections to one another, to justice, to peace, and to sustainable hope. My images aim to acknowledge and nourish that spirit, and in the countenance of multi-determined personal and global trauma, illumine, vivify and remind us of our potentially indivisible connections.

The following body of artwork is an investigative query and reflection about what it means to paint with hands borrowed by *Spirit*, and brushes dipped in its love and force of interminable mystery. It aims to highlight the epistemology of an inner knowledge that defies the rational mind and ofttimes dwells in places of esoteric ecstasy. This body of work aims to speak a language of awe and respect, of tenderness and connection to one another and the divinity between and among realms of existences.

In states of grace, the paintings bring messages from a place of profundity, a place where words and identifiable representation lie outside of the language of knowingness. In that place, movement, visual tension and flow speak a tongue of the heart that transcends limitations to evoke a fusion of artistry with inner character, and cosmology toward intents of global understanding, and beyond.

Heaven and Earth

Between divine and mundane
living links interconnect
Ever-weaving loops
meander with
Ouroborus infinity

acrylic and oil pastels
48 x 60 inches

Page 74

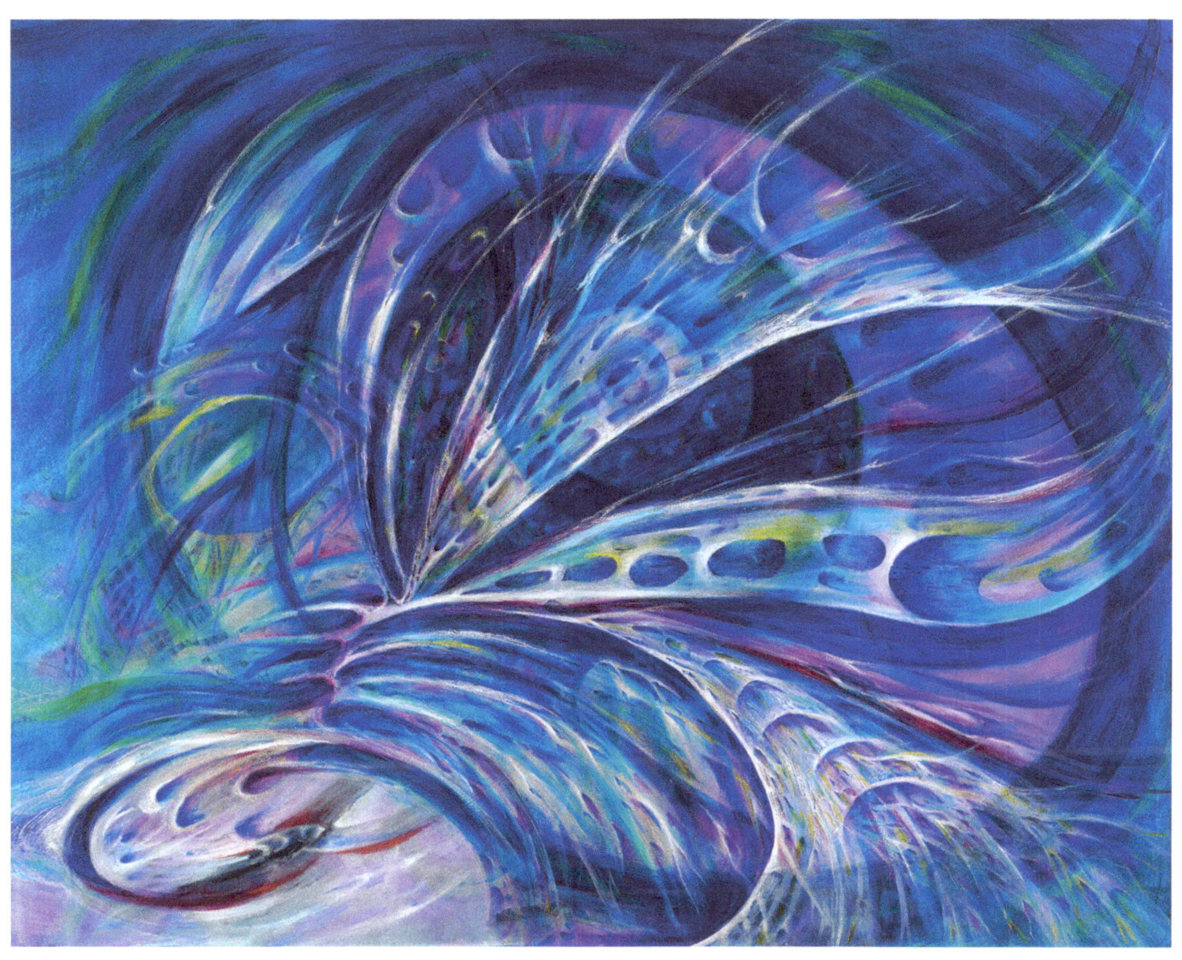

PLATE 28

Breath of Divinity I

The obvious isn't
Presenting differently
Moving from here to other
Breath nourishes and sustains
Keeping perpetual change afoot

acrylic and oil pastels
48 x 45 inches

Page 76

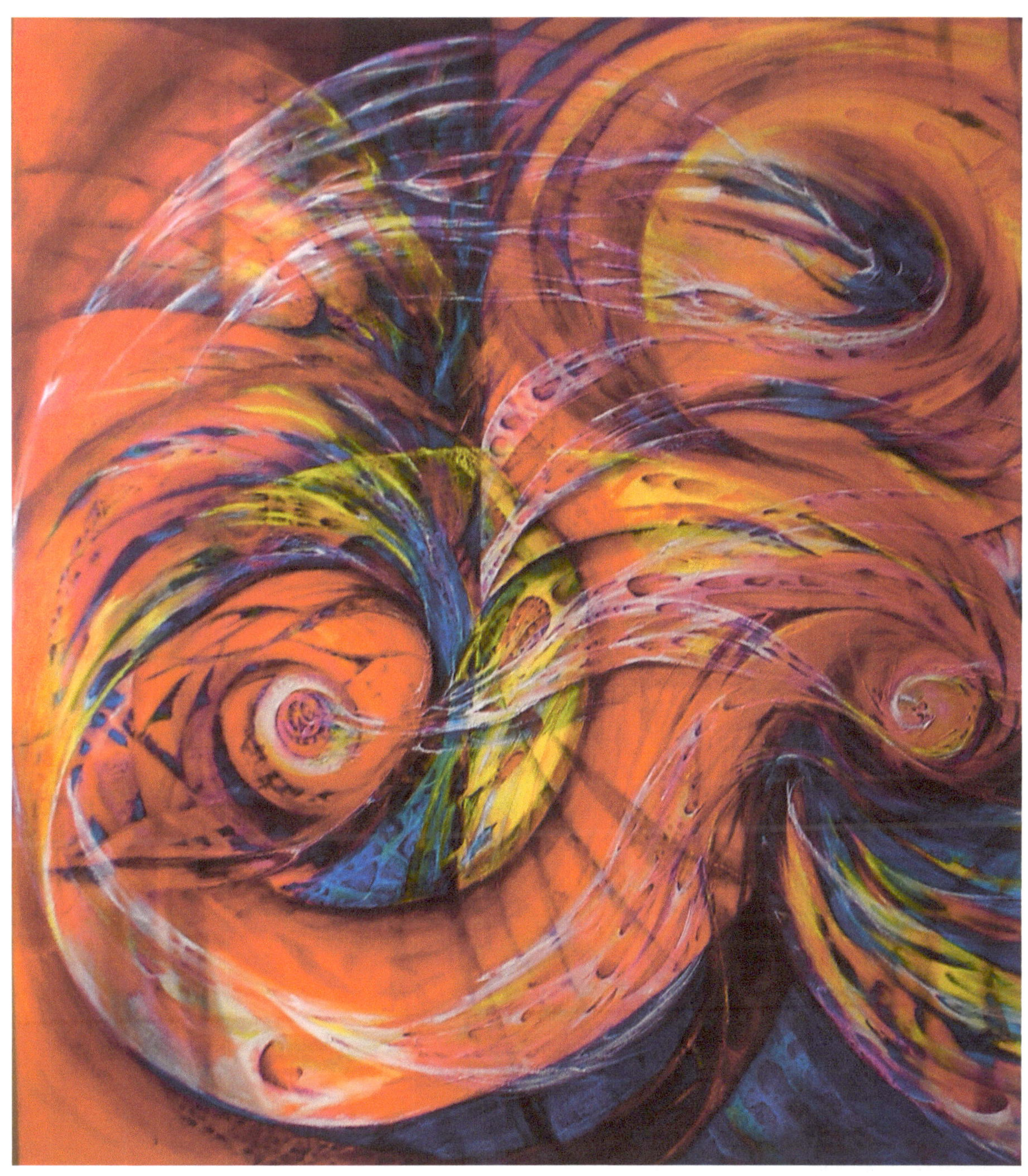

PLATE 29

Breath of Divinity II

Sustenance gathers
on its way to becoming,
to expressing some powerful,
wonderful otherness

acrylic and oil pastels
48 x 60 inches

Page 78

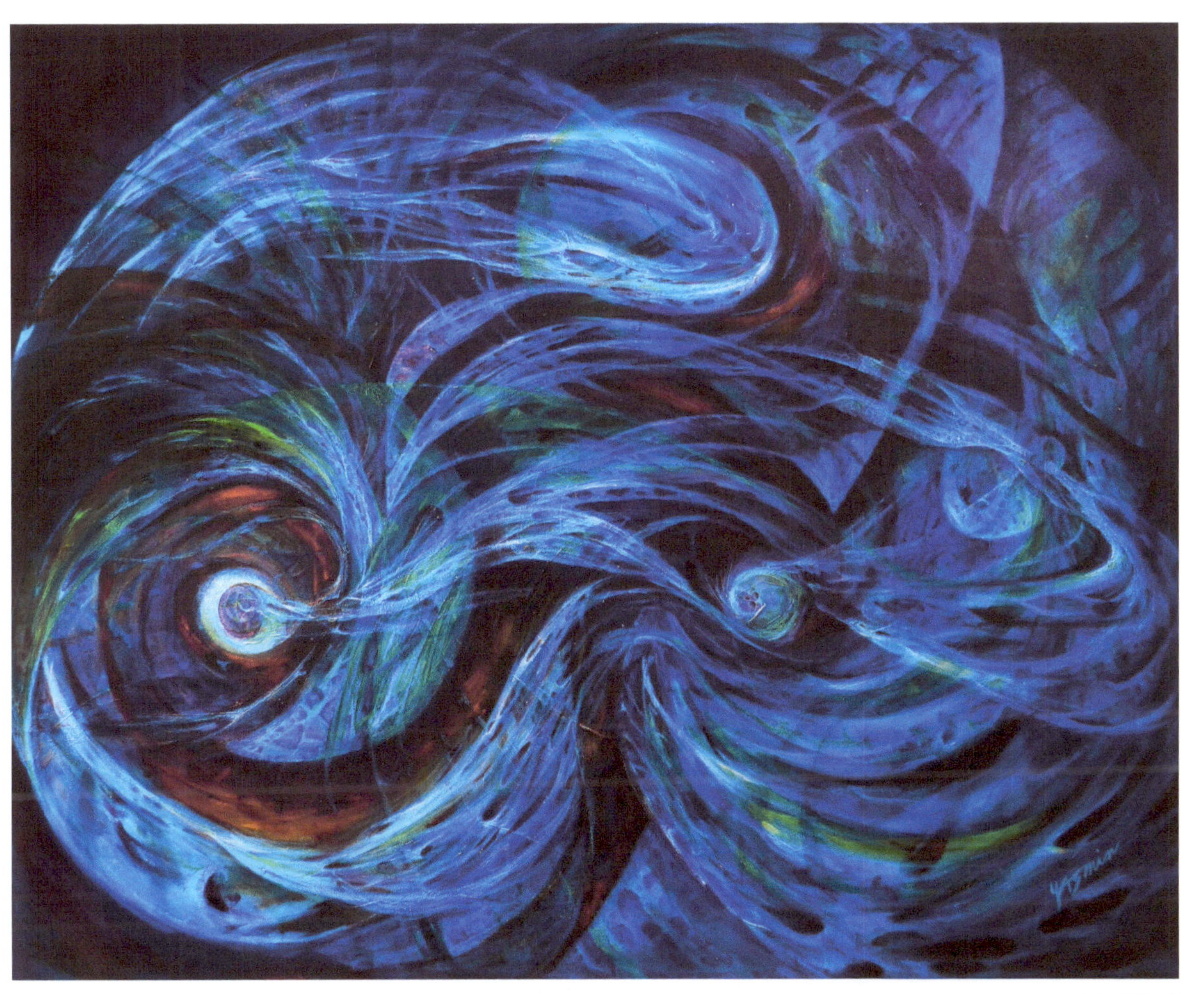

PLATE 30

Looking Around

I looked around, Sweet Pea,
and you were gone
Gone yet not departed
Steadfast in remaining
while I learned
new dance steps
in the business of living
without your rhythm

acrylic and oil pastels
50 x 32 inches

Page 80

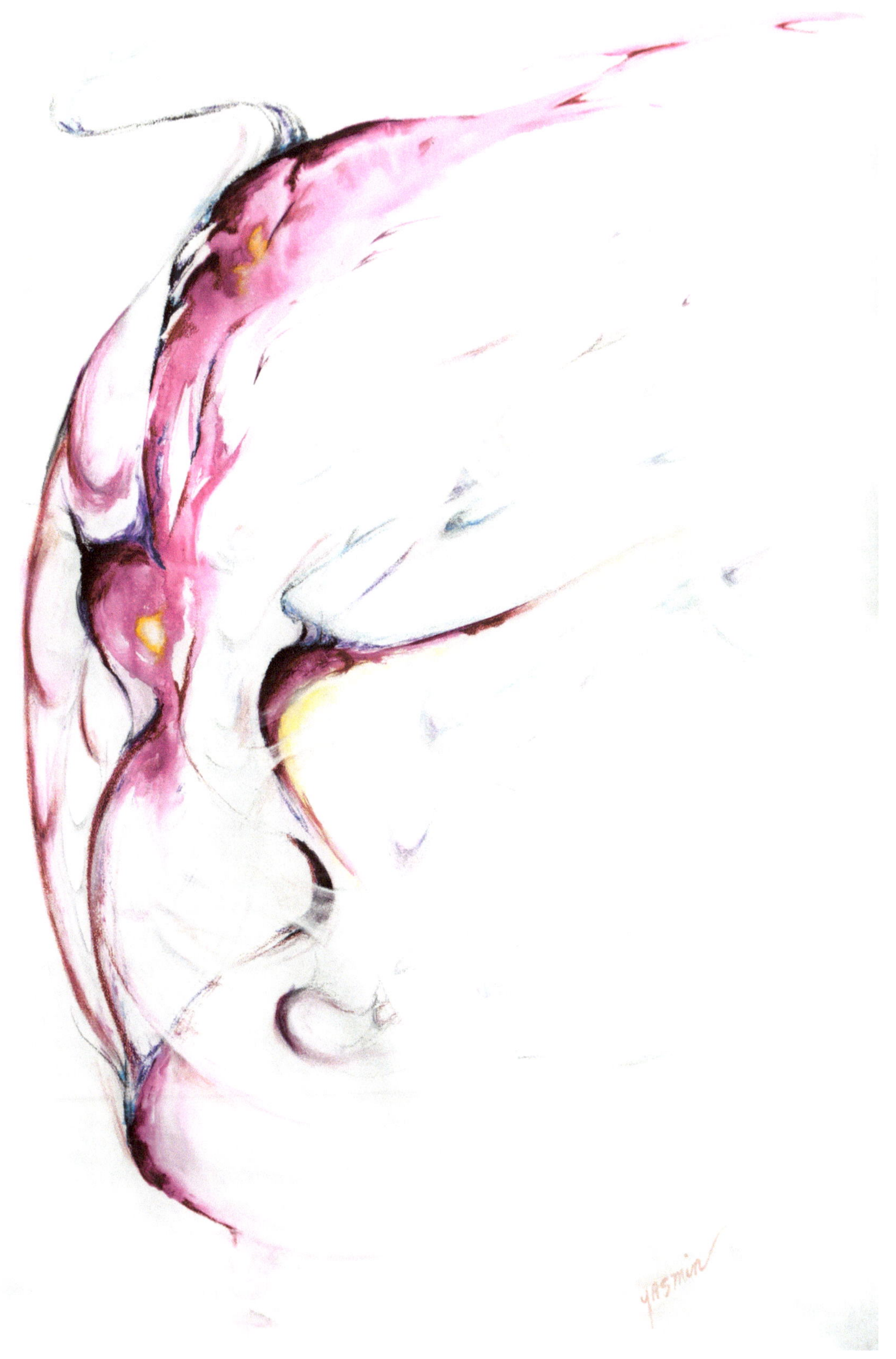

PLATE 31

Soul Soothing

At first
all I could see
and sense were the cavernous depths of emptiness
Grace visited gently
Memories filled spaces
Wonder reinsinuated itself
holding hands
with smiles and laughter and life

acrylic and oil pastels
40 x 30 inches

Page 82

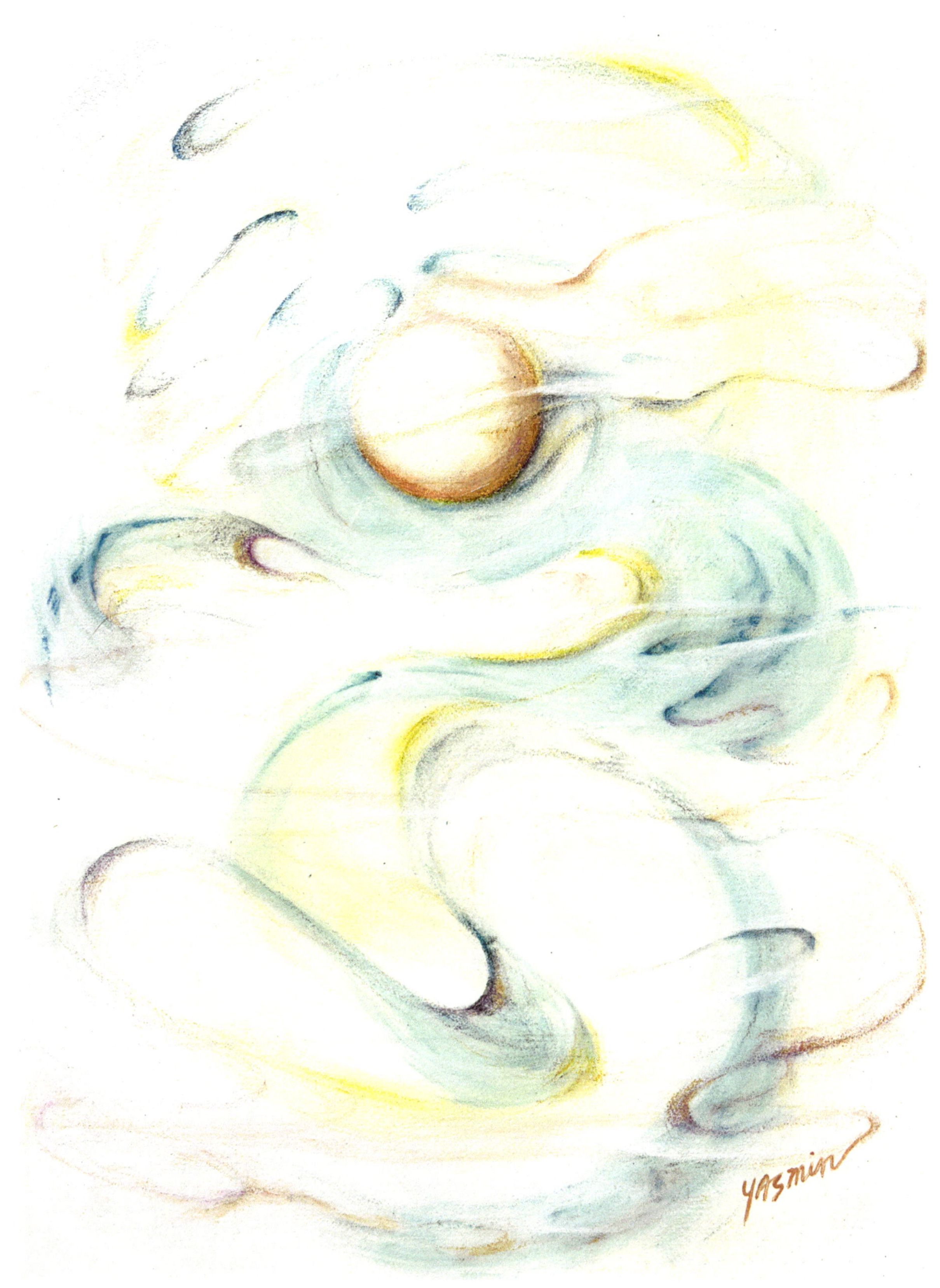

PLATE 32

Diptych: Sister Spirit

With words ofttimes unspoken
we speak psyches
satiated with loving
Knowing gifts wondrous
and expansive

acrylic and oil pastels
40 x 60 inches
collection of Maria Julia Garcia-Caron

Page 84

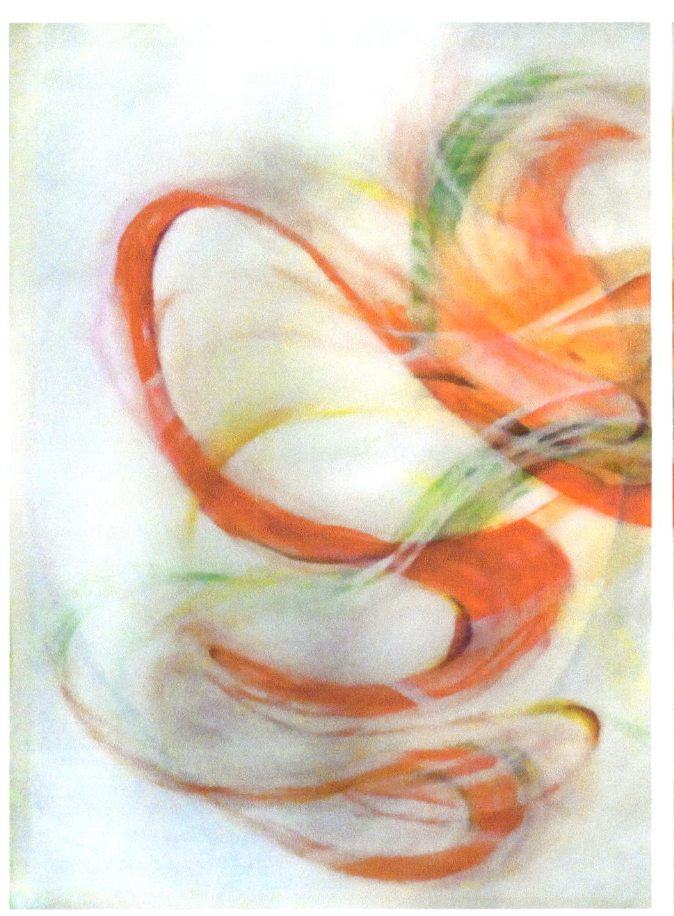
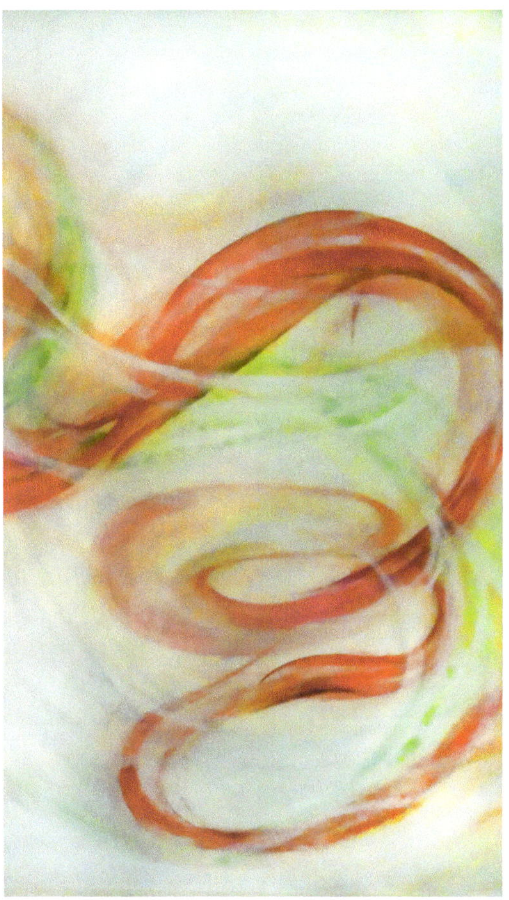

PLATE 33

Spirit Breath

Breathe
Life changes
Gentle breezes anoint
with expansive grace
Beatific bliss
intoxicates
without effort

acrylic and oil
40 x 50 inches
collection of Maria Julia Garcia-Caron

Page 86

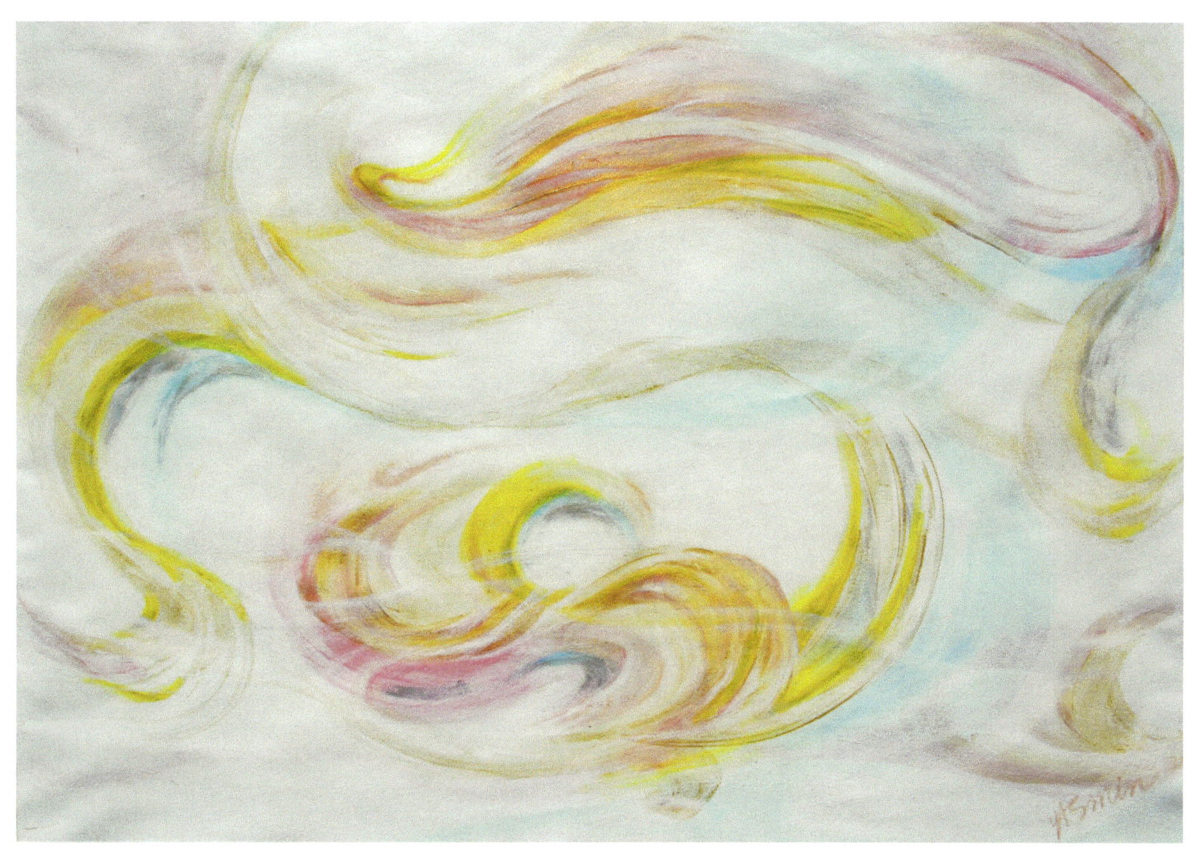

PLATE 34

Diptych: Anew

Grieving heart
finding new ways
to rediscover joy

acrylic and oil
40 x 48 inches

Page 88

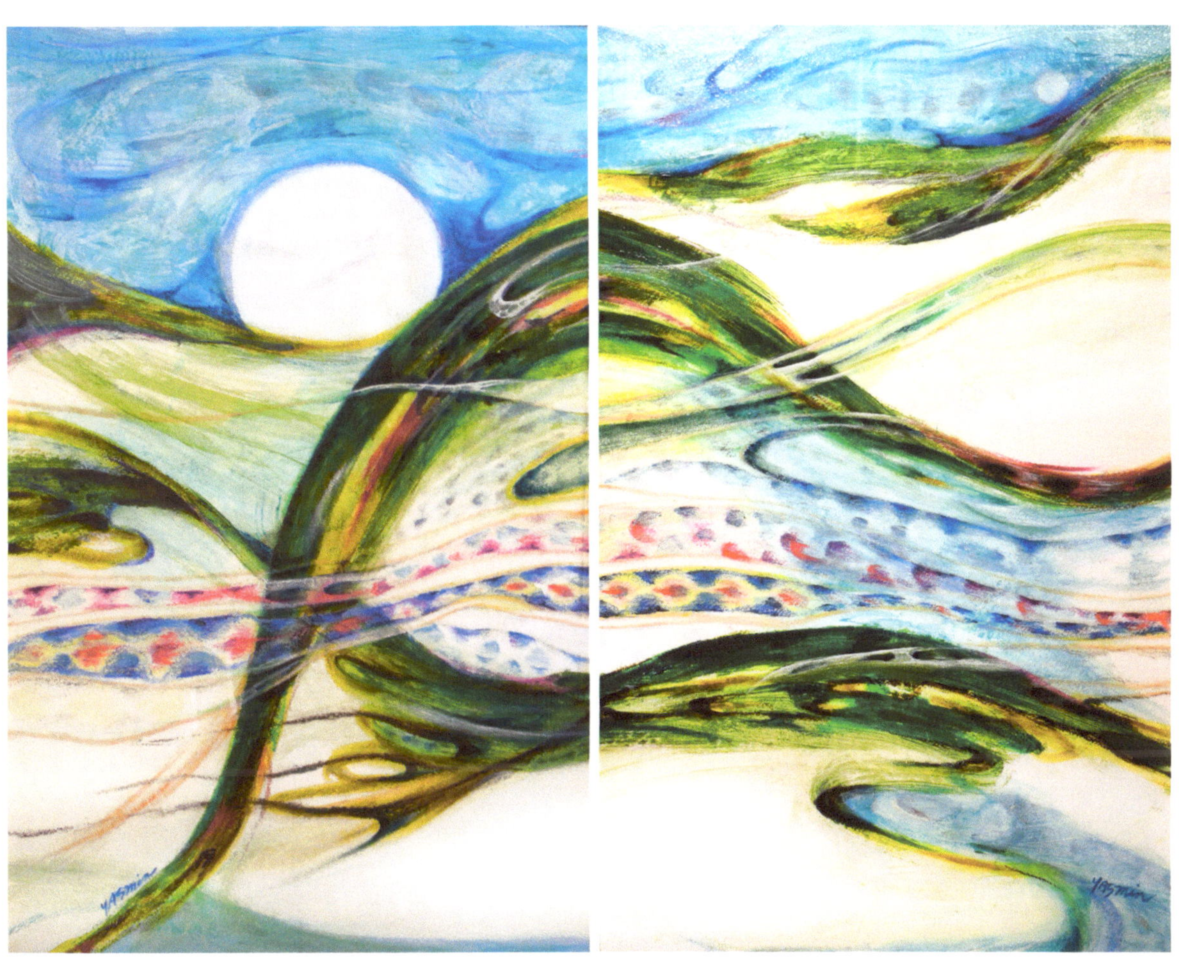

PLATE 35

Iwa Ni Mopé

Gratitude blesses the grateful
Opens ways of knowing
seeing and being in
the experience of life
with neither succumbing to its weight
nor crushing
others with our power

acrylic and oil pastels
60 x 48 inches

Page 90

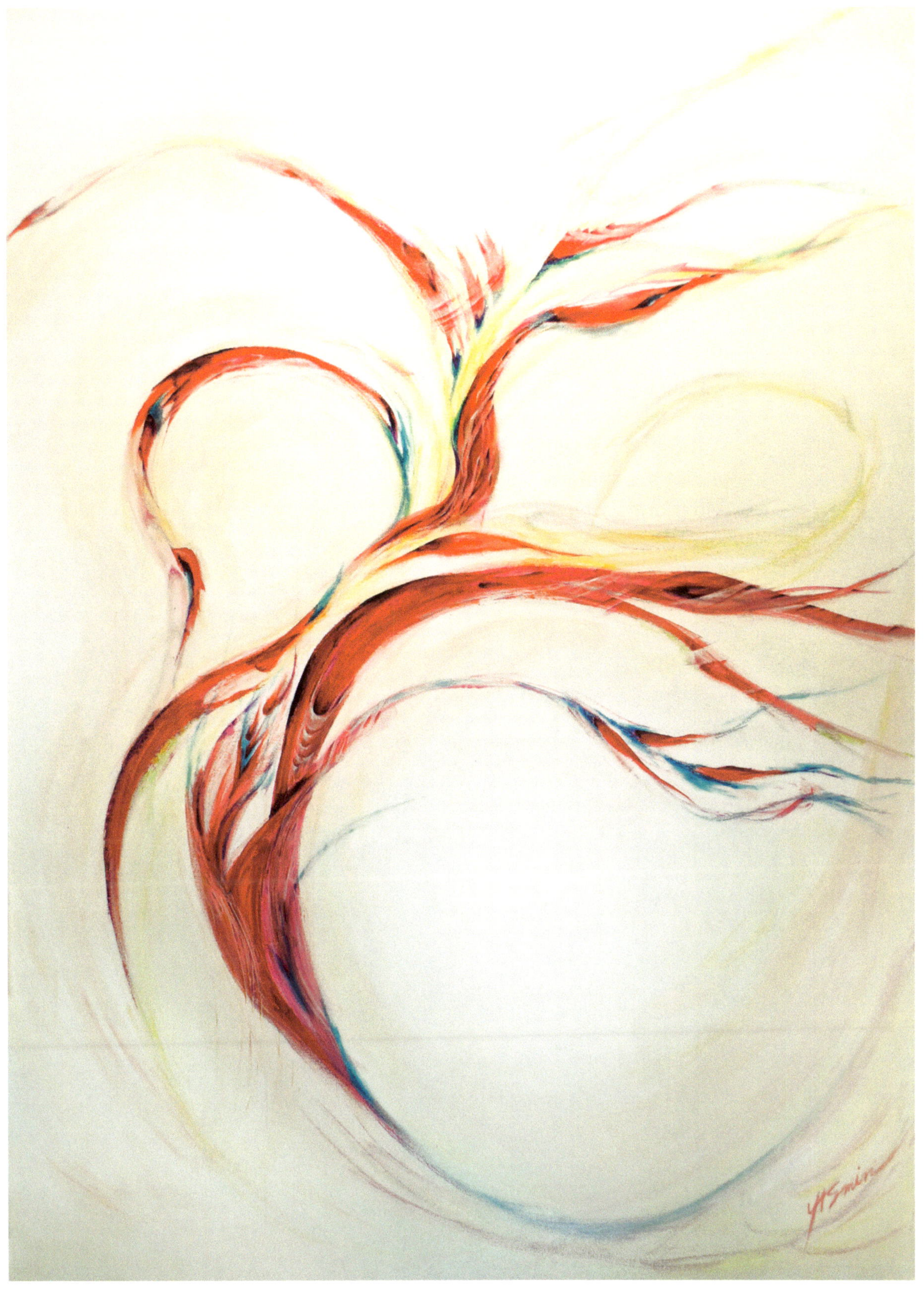

PLATE 36

Gentle Breeze

Sun kissed breezes
anoint the soul
with honey salved breath

acrylic and oil pastels
60 x 48 inches

Page 92

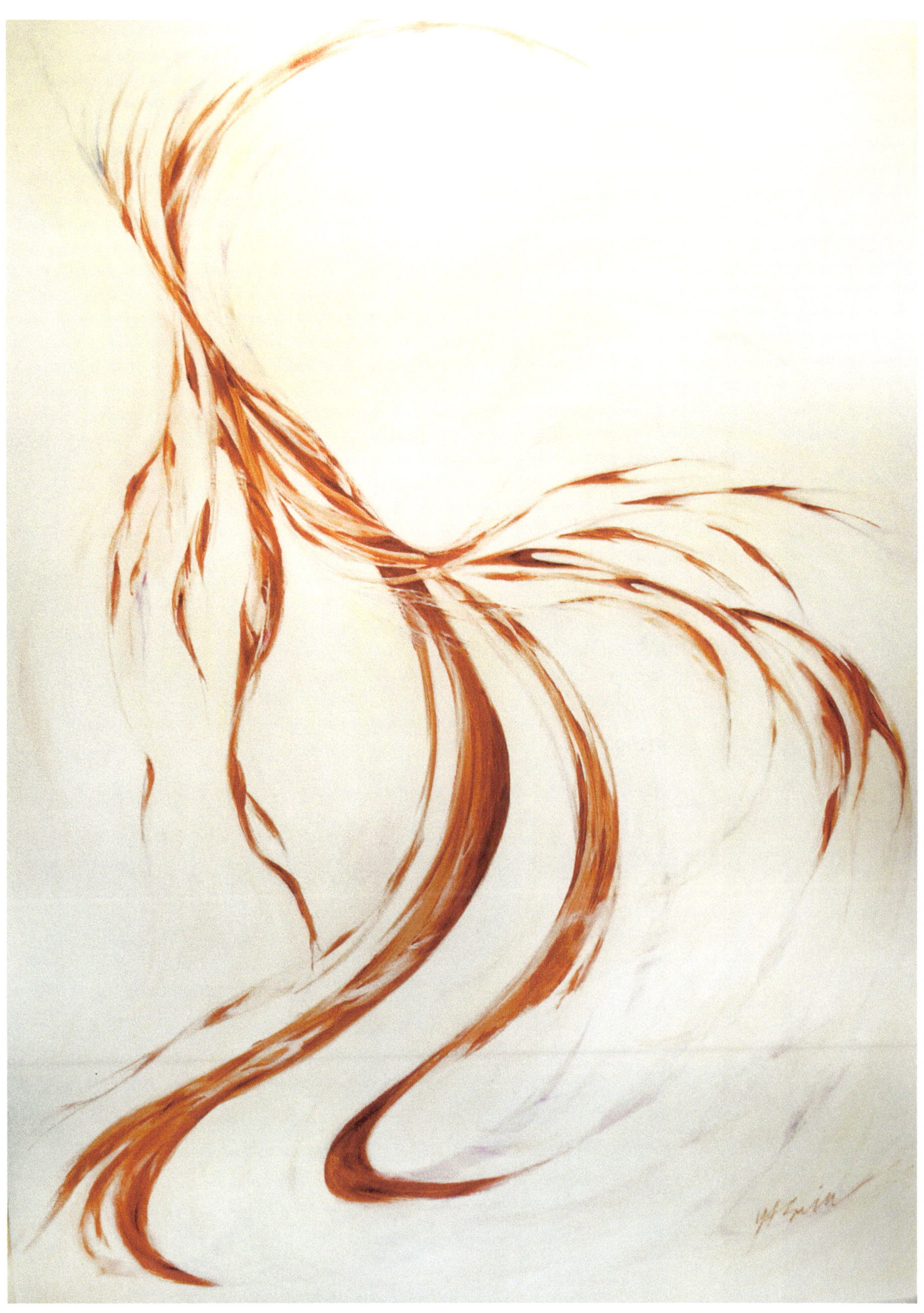

PLATE 37

Path Finding

Making roads
Following paths
orchestrated from within
towards confluences
of peace commingled
with justice …
capacious and inclusive

acrylic and oil pastels
40 x 30 inches

Page 94

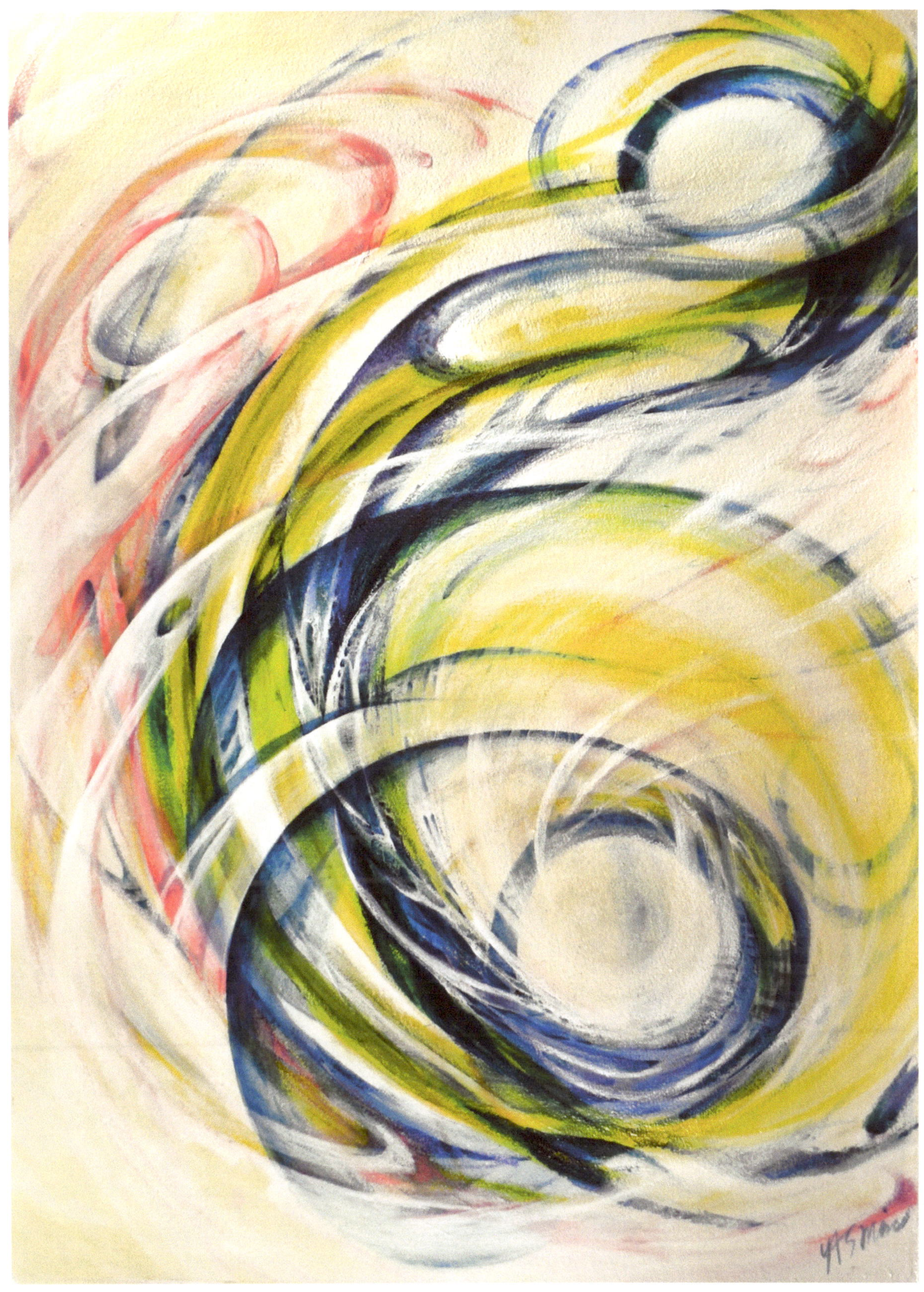

PLATE 38

Spirit Breath II

Glimpses of joy
Everyday
a meditation revealed
an injury made whole

acrylic and oil
40 x 50 inches

Page 96

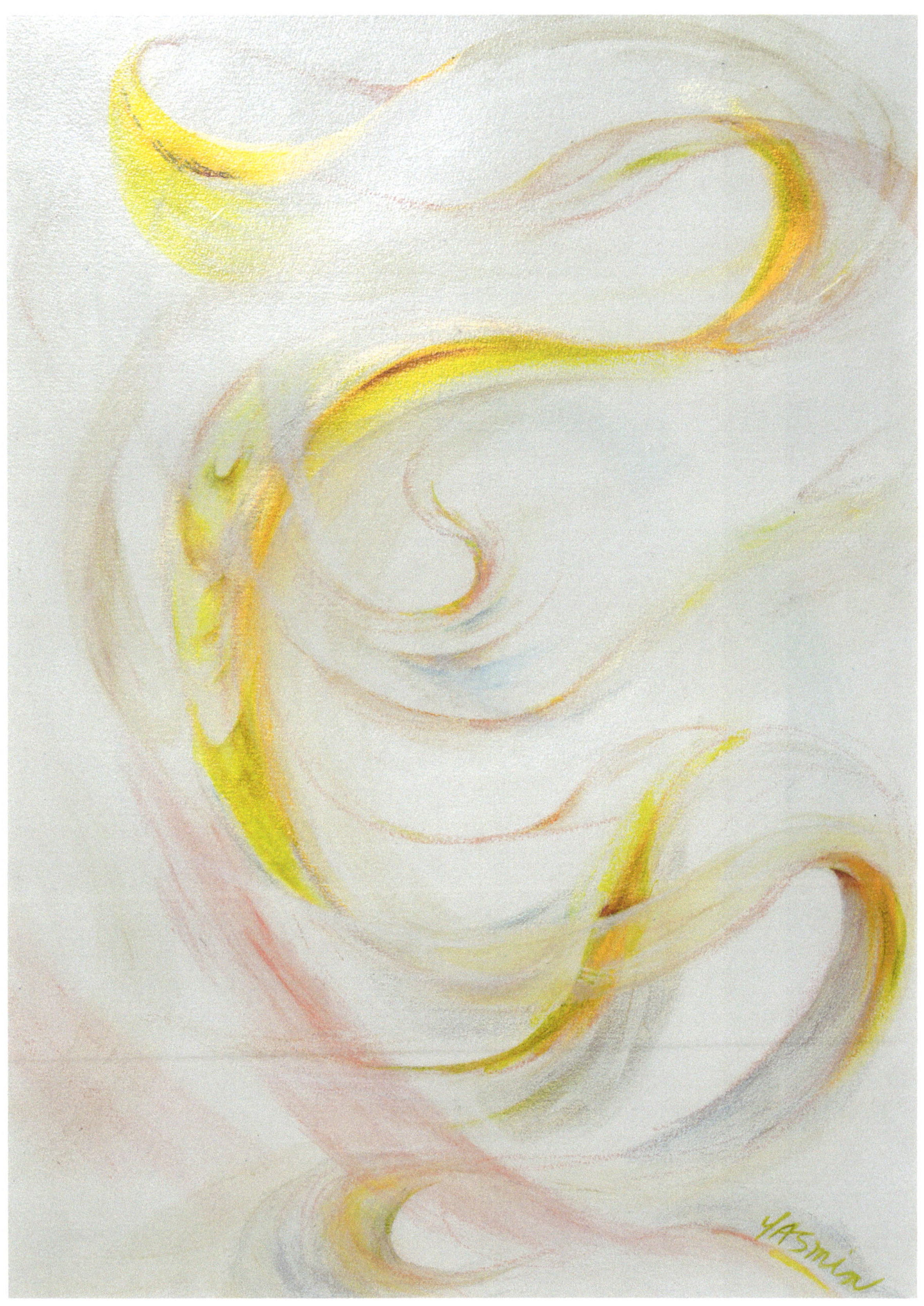

PLATE 39

Journeying: Troubled Waters

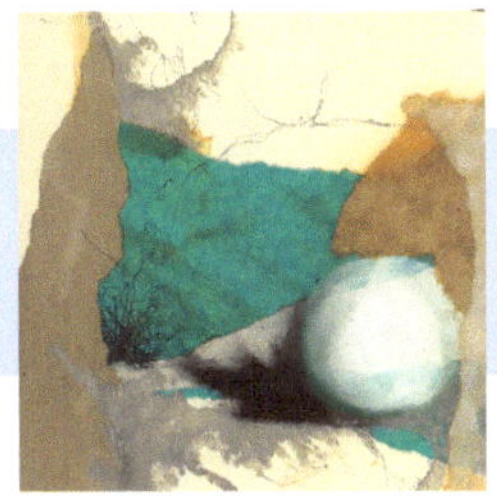

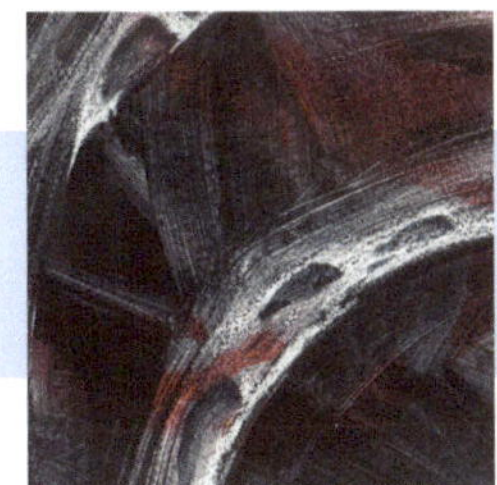

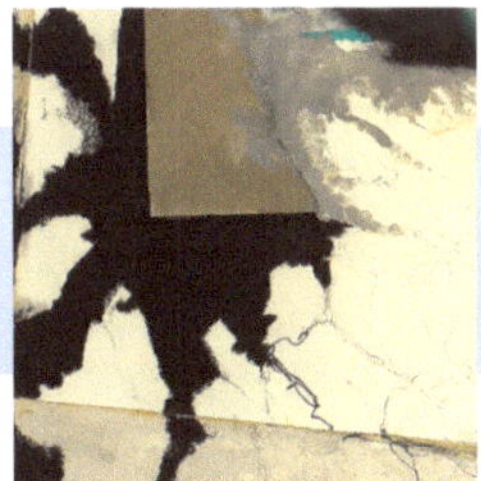

Concurrent to beatific flows that surround us, troubled waters reside, some of which loom in defiance of the parameters of decency. Sometimes people, institutions and governments live outside of clarity, conscience and consciousness, and sometimes within clear intents of power and domination over other people, and all that lies within creation.

My work as an artist also serves as a platform for amplified voice against oppressions, against the genocides of cultures, the ravages against Mother Earth and the assails against the sacred. I think it important to speak our truths even in the countenance of discomfort and danger, and perhaps specifically because the art world, academia and cultural institutions ofttimes function as oppressive regimes in terms of their hegemonic colonialization of information, culture and representation of nonconforming artists.

Bones of Dar Fur

Invaders come
Destruction moans in the dry bones
of the fallen
Felled for differences in experiencing
Spirit and for wearing faces other than
the plunderers, armed with notions of
superiority and deadened hearts

acrylic and oil pastels
22 x 30 inches

Page 100

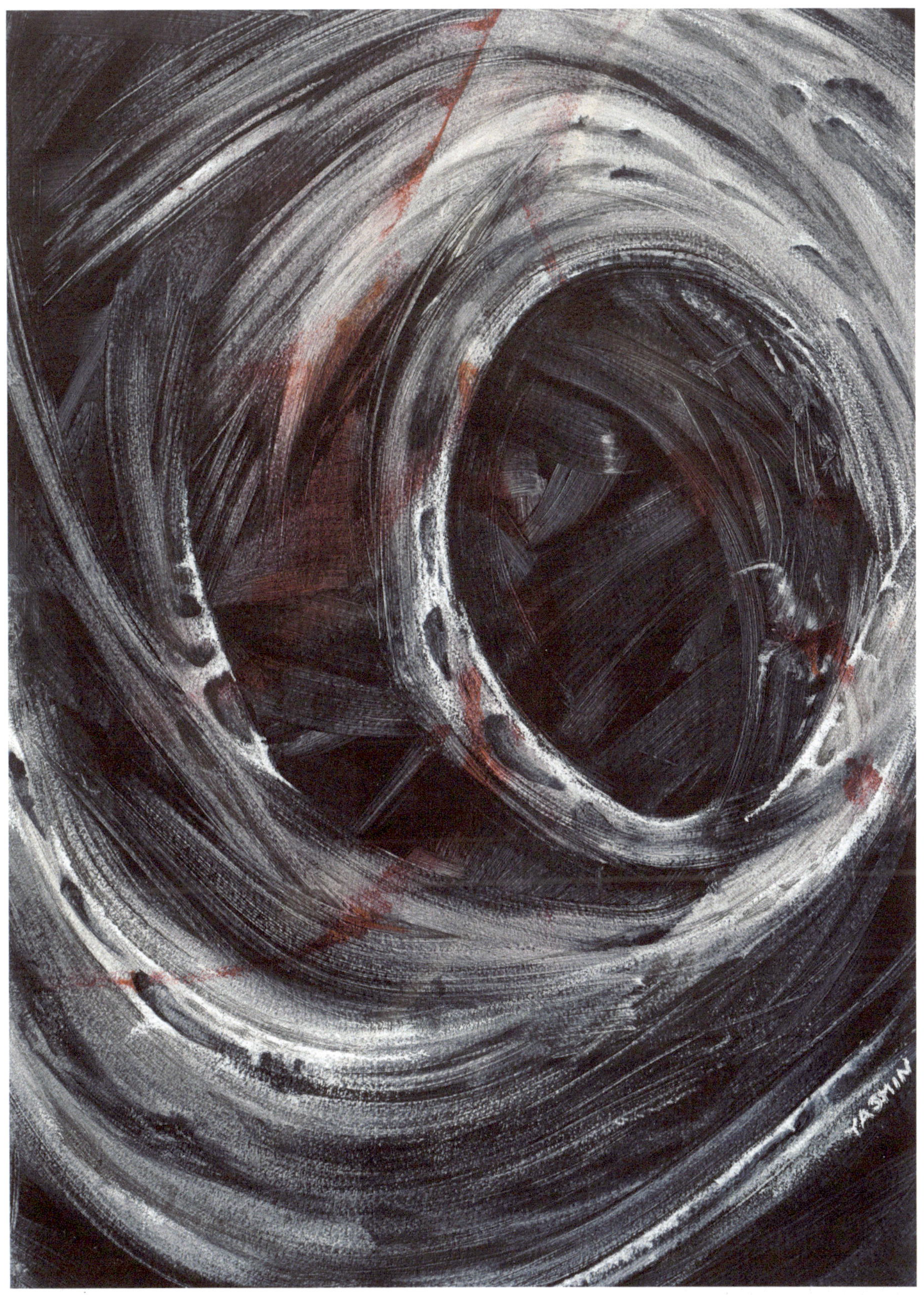

PLATE 40

Ghost Wails

Following the slavers' ships Atlantic Ocean
sharks changed their migration and feeding patterns
for over one hundred years

Through hollowed bones
African ghost-chants moan
from the depths of the Atlantic
wailing for an end of antilife horrors

acrylic and oil pastels
22 x 30 inches

Page 102

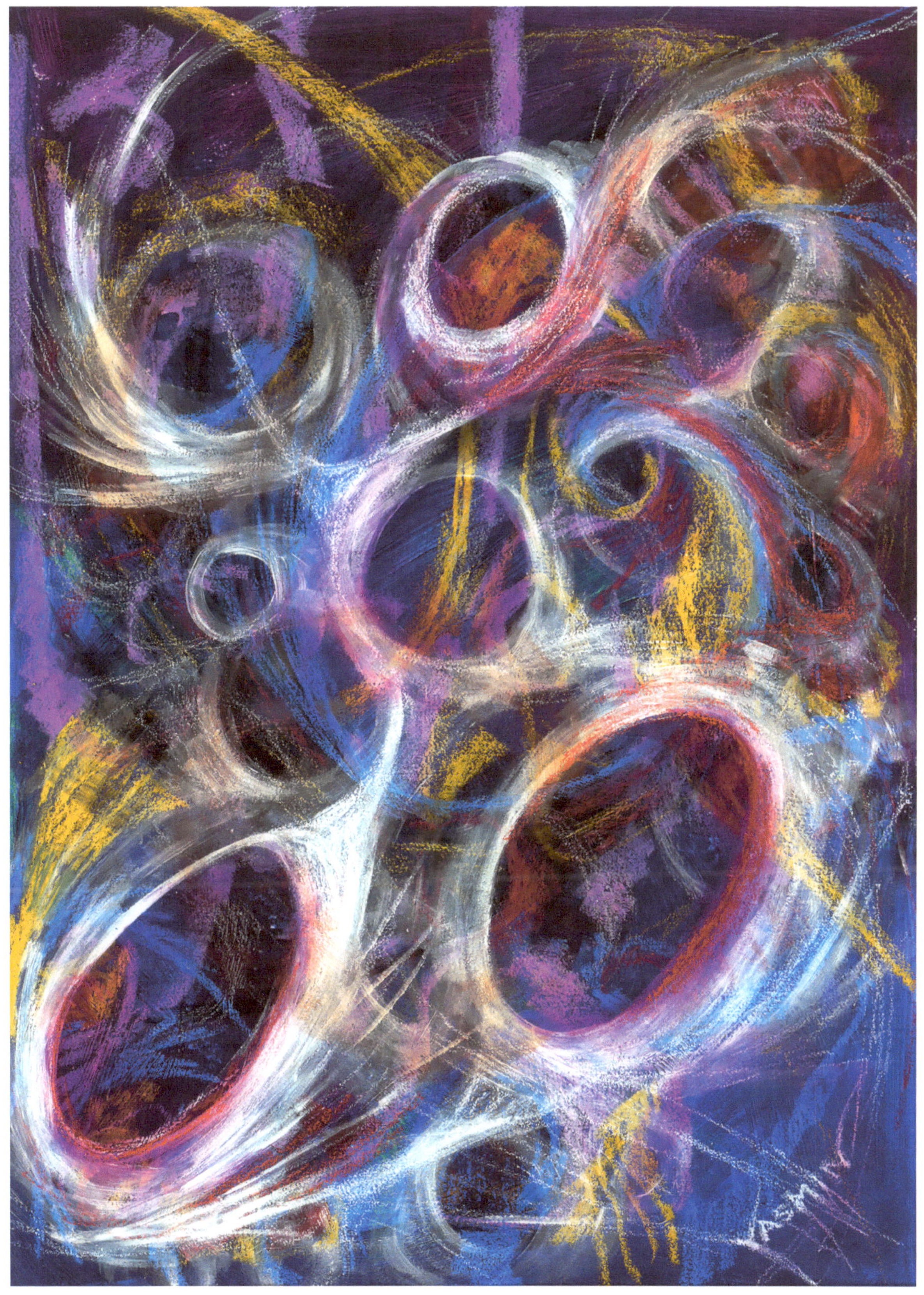

PLATE 41

Bound: An outcry against female circumcision

Courageous cultural dialogues require brave acts of committed people

mixed media—oil pastels, acrylic, India ink
22 x 30 inches

Page 104

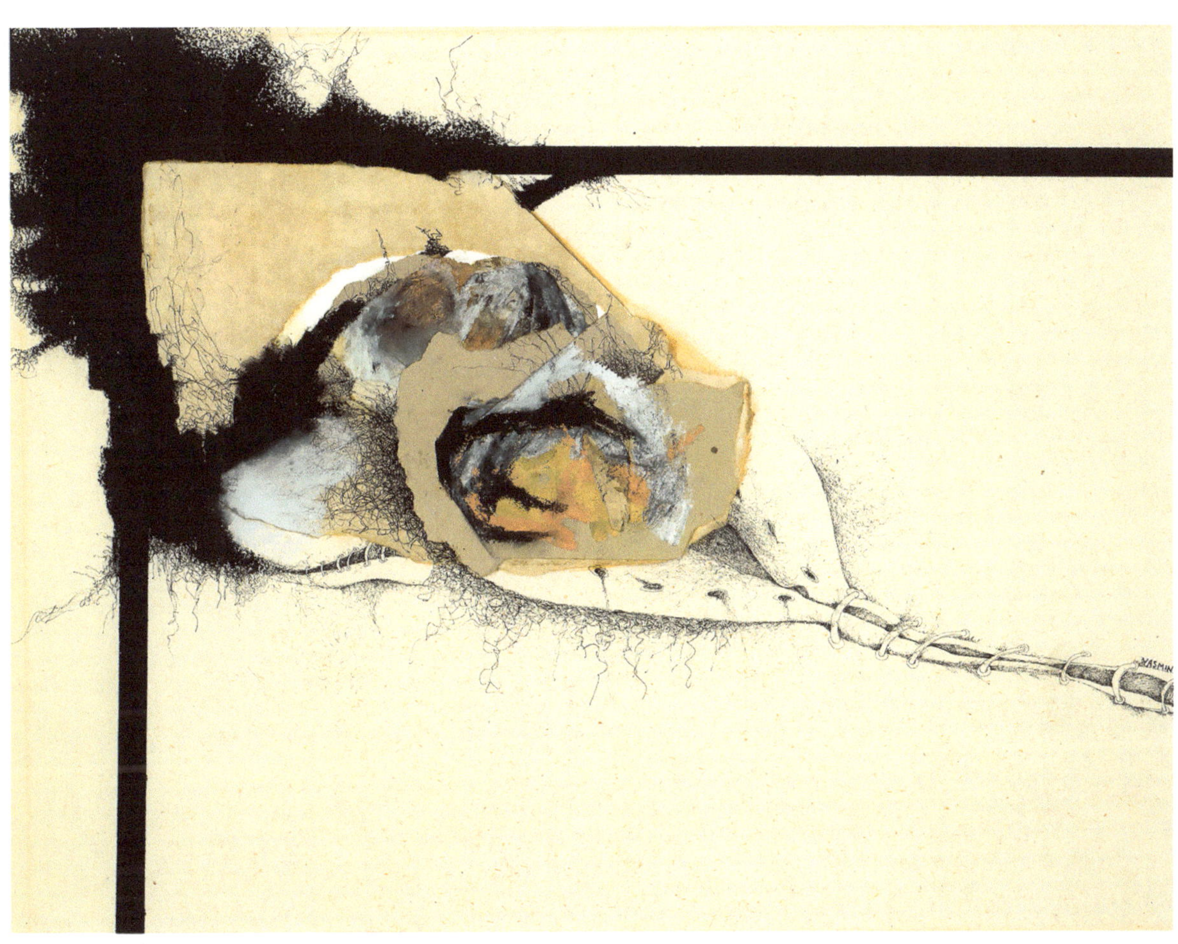

PLATE 42

Unbound

Betrayal not of culture
to say no,
to claim the unwrapped gift
as mine to know

mixed media—oil pastels, acrylic, India ink
22 x 30 inches

Page 106

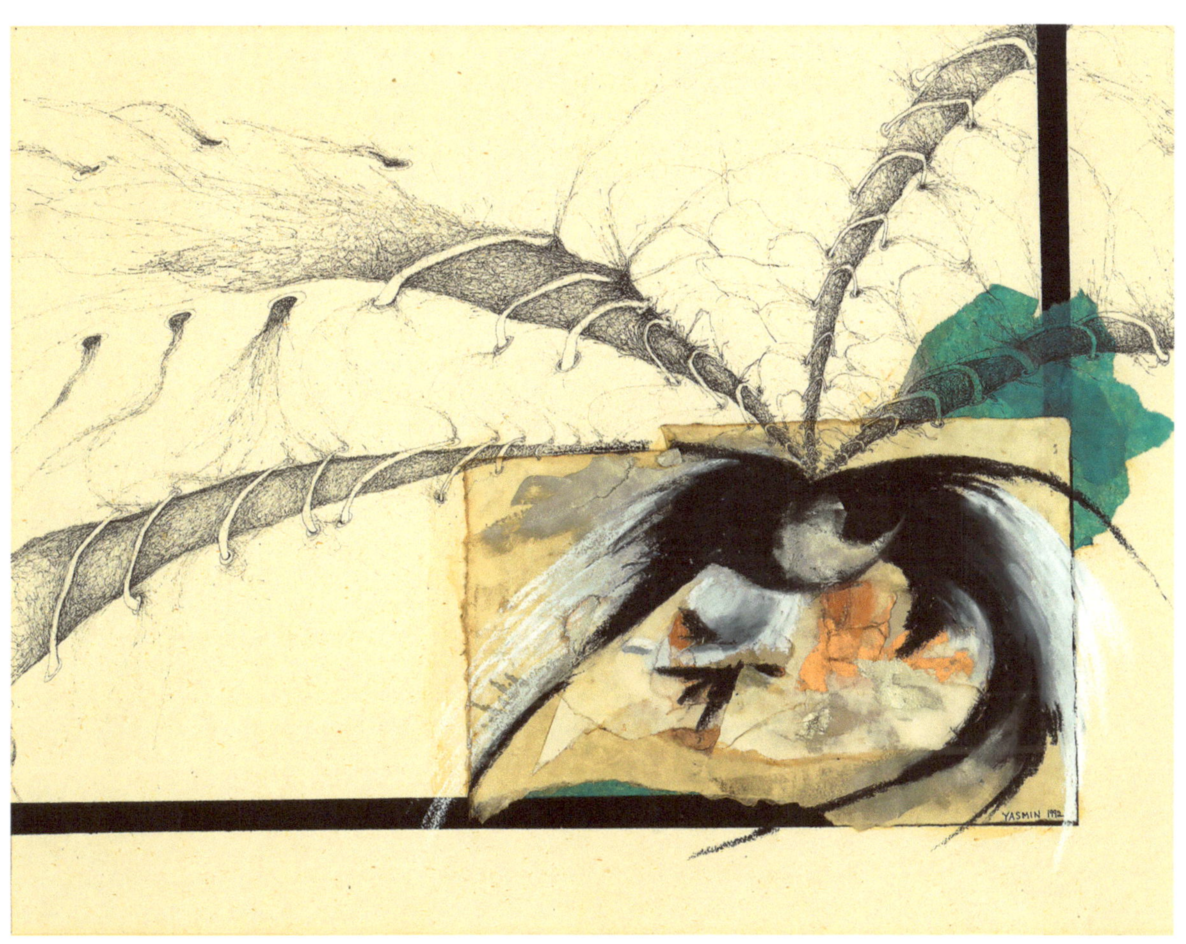

PLATE 43

Joy Claimed

Sacredness of body
a divine gift
defined neither
by the limitations of man
nor antiquity
of culture

mixed media—oil pastels, acrylic, India ink
22 x 30 inches

Page 108

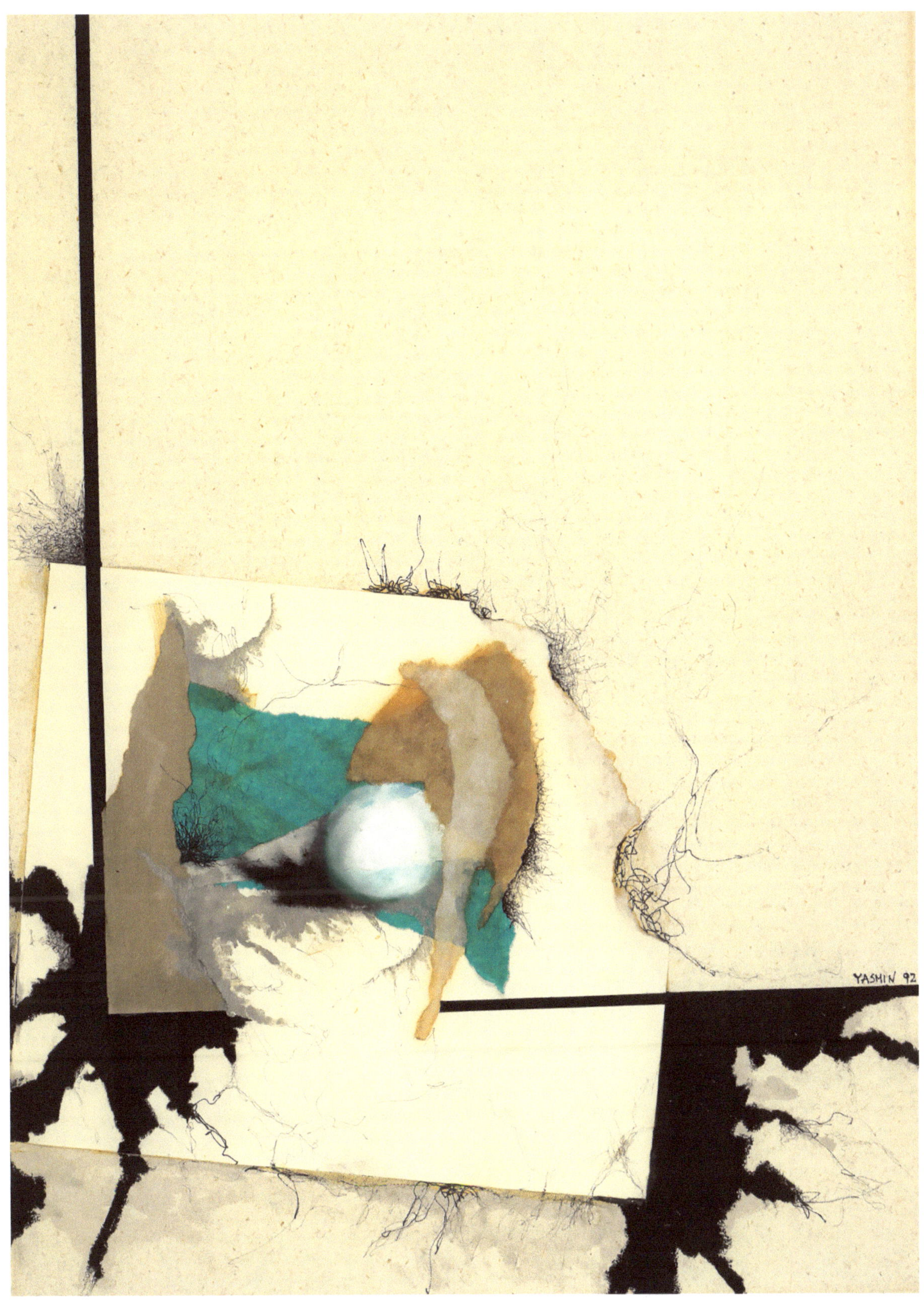

PLATE 44

Journeying: Justice or Just-us

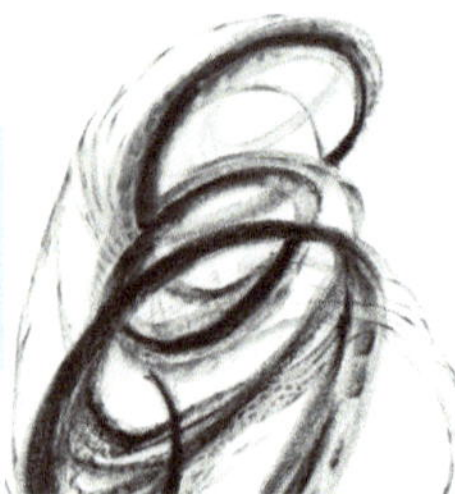
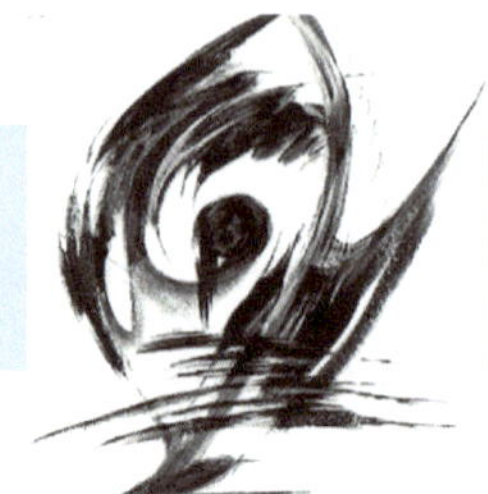
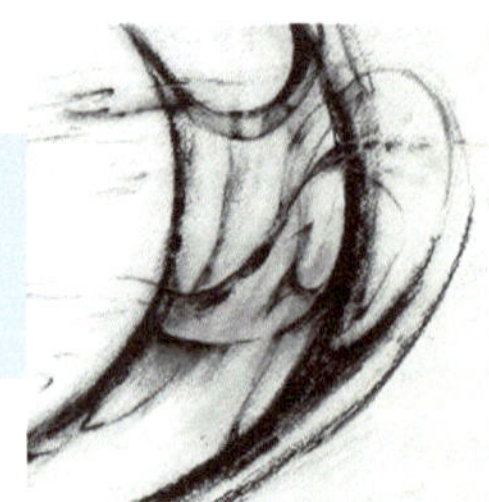

For Oscar Grant, Jonathan Ferrell, Trayvon Martin, Jordan Davis, Michael Brown and all who walk, have walked and will walk in their told and untold realities.

This body of work is specifically about a particular vein of inequities regarding people of African ancestry, in the United States, and concurrently, a universal representation of solidarity with all peoples laboring under injustices.

Justice or Just-us
is not a single subject
single peoples' cry.
We need a language to name the inclusivity of madnesses
that interconnect and collocate injustices--
and not solely the human-to-human degradations.
We disparage that which dehumanizes, but what common language includes
human assails against nature? Perhaps we need to explore paradigms
of egalitarianism that shift from the anthropocentric and ethnocentric
worldviews—
the basis of which promotes human domination
and notions of class, gender, language and religious superiority.

In my lens of perception
the same violence that wiped out the gentle Tainos, and fierce Caribs from
Española is the same violence that obsesses our children.

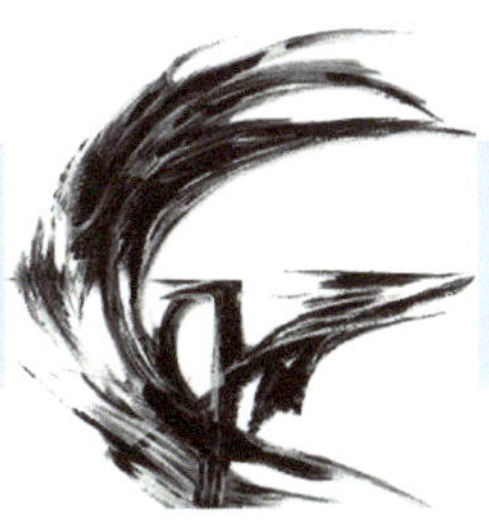 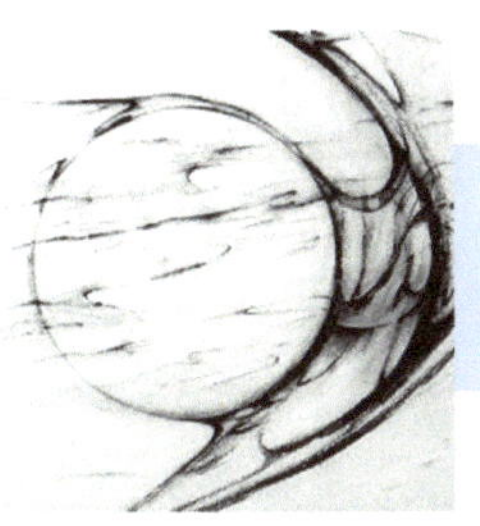 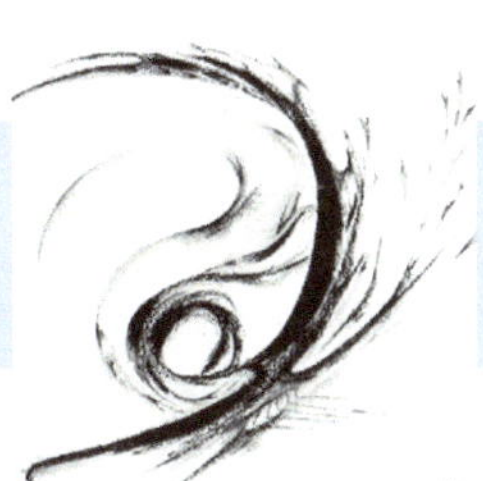

The same madness of hatred and domination that plundered the Americas and
wrapped indigenous peoples in smallpox-infested blankets
is the same vileness that loads bullets into guns held by our children.
The same avarice, the same entitlement that colonized Chinese laborers and
later burned their communities to the ground as they slept in their beds at night
is the same vileness that has our children enter schools loaded for hunting.
The same depravities that enslaved Africans in the US for over 300 years,
followed by 100 years of lynchings
is the same depravity that pulls the triggers of children-to-children violence.
The roots of inculcated violence
create gangs
situate border patrols on stolen land
create familial violence, sex trafficking
Ponzi schemes, and uncountable structural abuses
What is done to one
visits all.
Justice or just-us
is about those named and unnamed
fingers on the triggers.

Where *Stand Your Ground* Means License to Hunt

Stand avowed
others derided
Stalk affirmed
take life unchided
Stand firm
if white and armed
Not so
if black
and stalked

acrylic
22 x 33 inches

Page 112

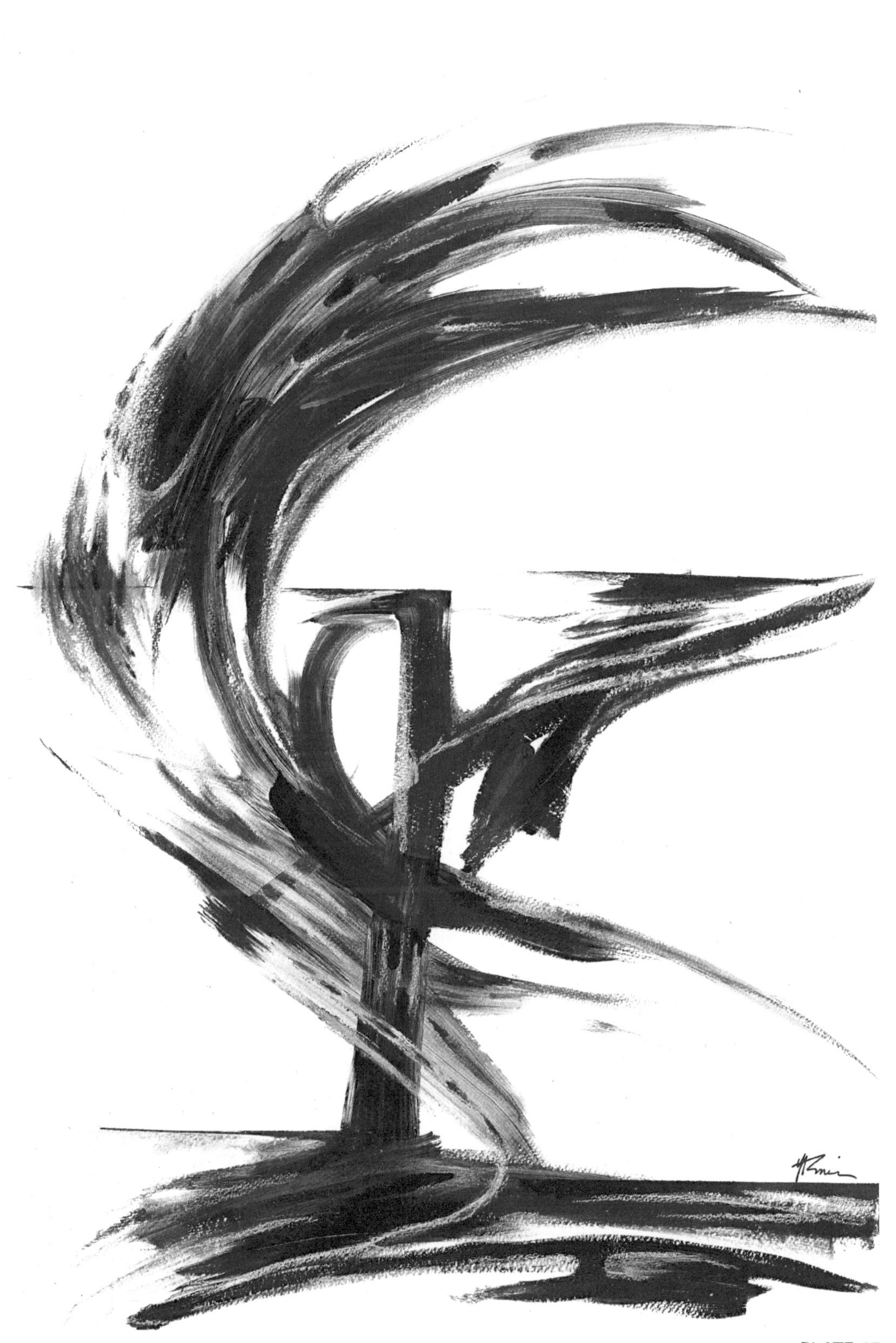

PLATE 45

Where *Wearing a 'Hoodie'* Means Wearing a Target

Scorn youth culture
youth bravado
if both housed
in black skin…
bull's eye looms
unbridled

acrylic
17 x 33 inches

Page 114

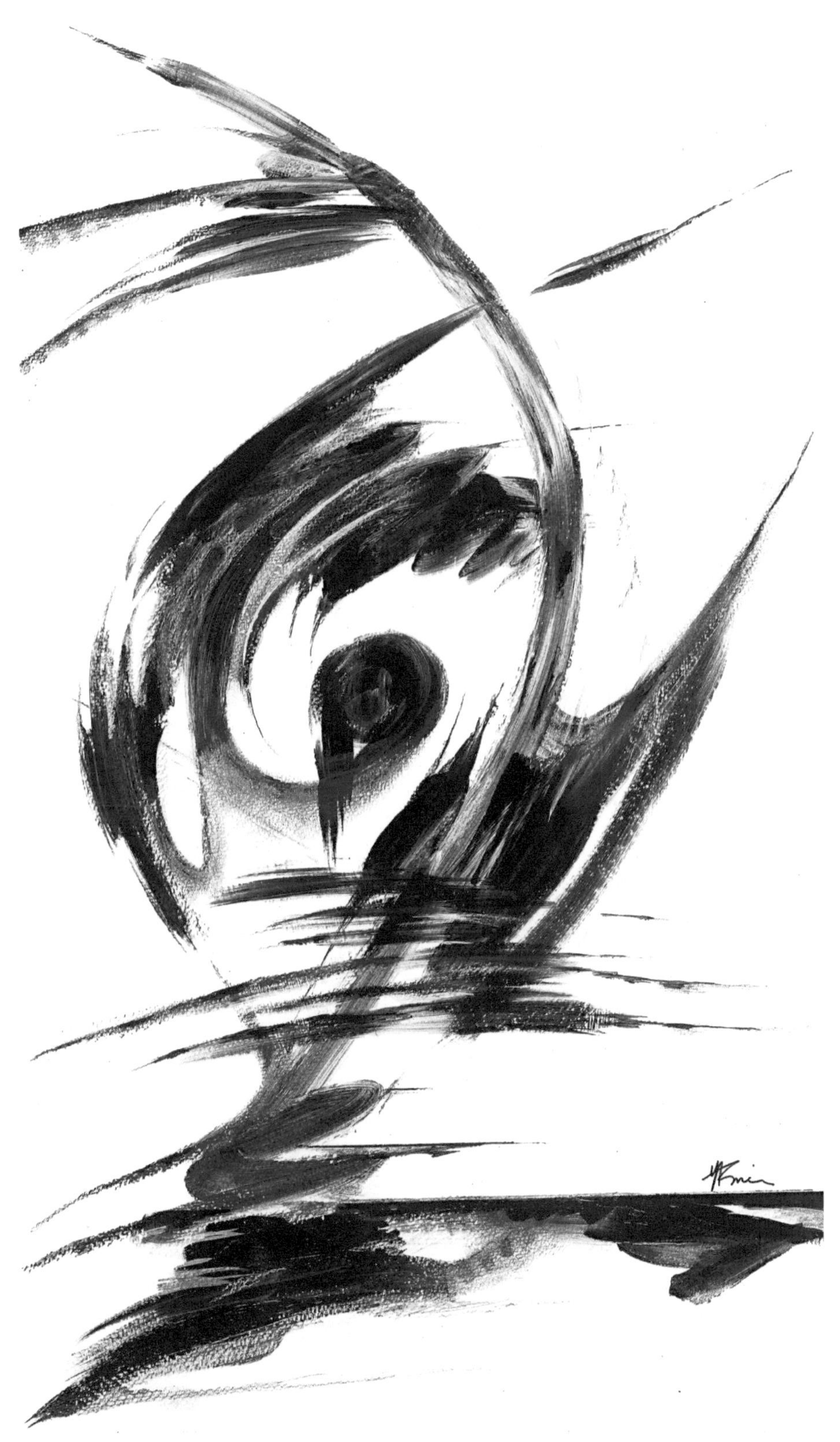

PLATE 46

Where *Maintaining Your Dignity* Means Lie Down and Die

If we must die
the poet penned
Young men heed
and mothers cry

acrylic
22 x 30 inches

Page 116

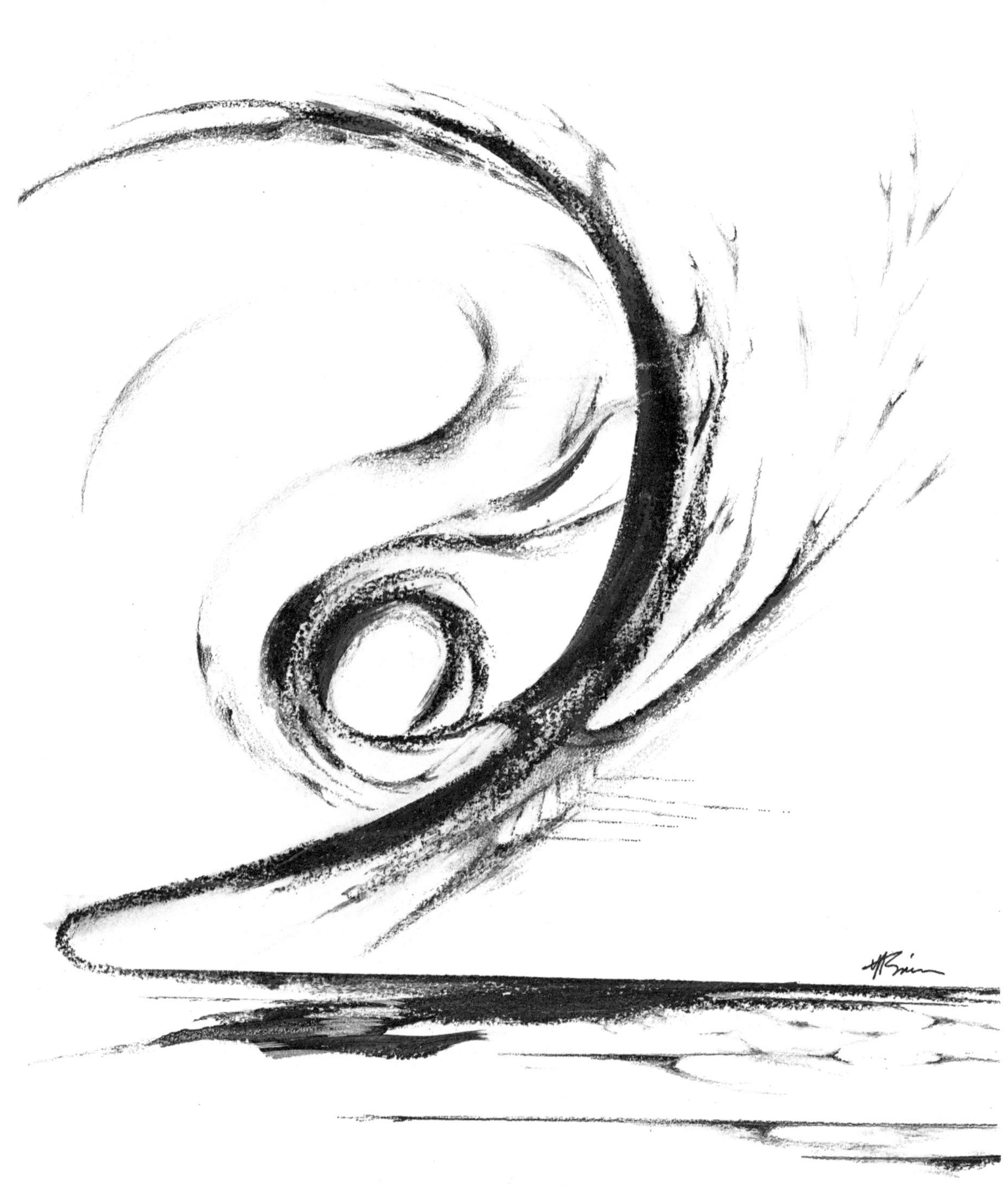

PLATE 47

Leaving the Table Of Humanity

Justice secures seats
at the table of humanity
In absence,
peace, no place of residence
no base on which to flourish
Restlessness
and rage abound

acrylic
26 x 36 inches

Page 118

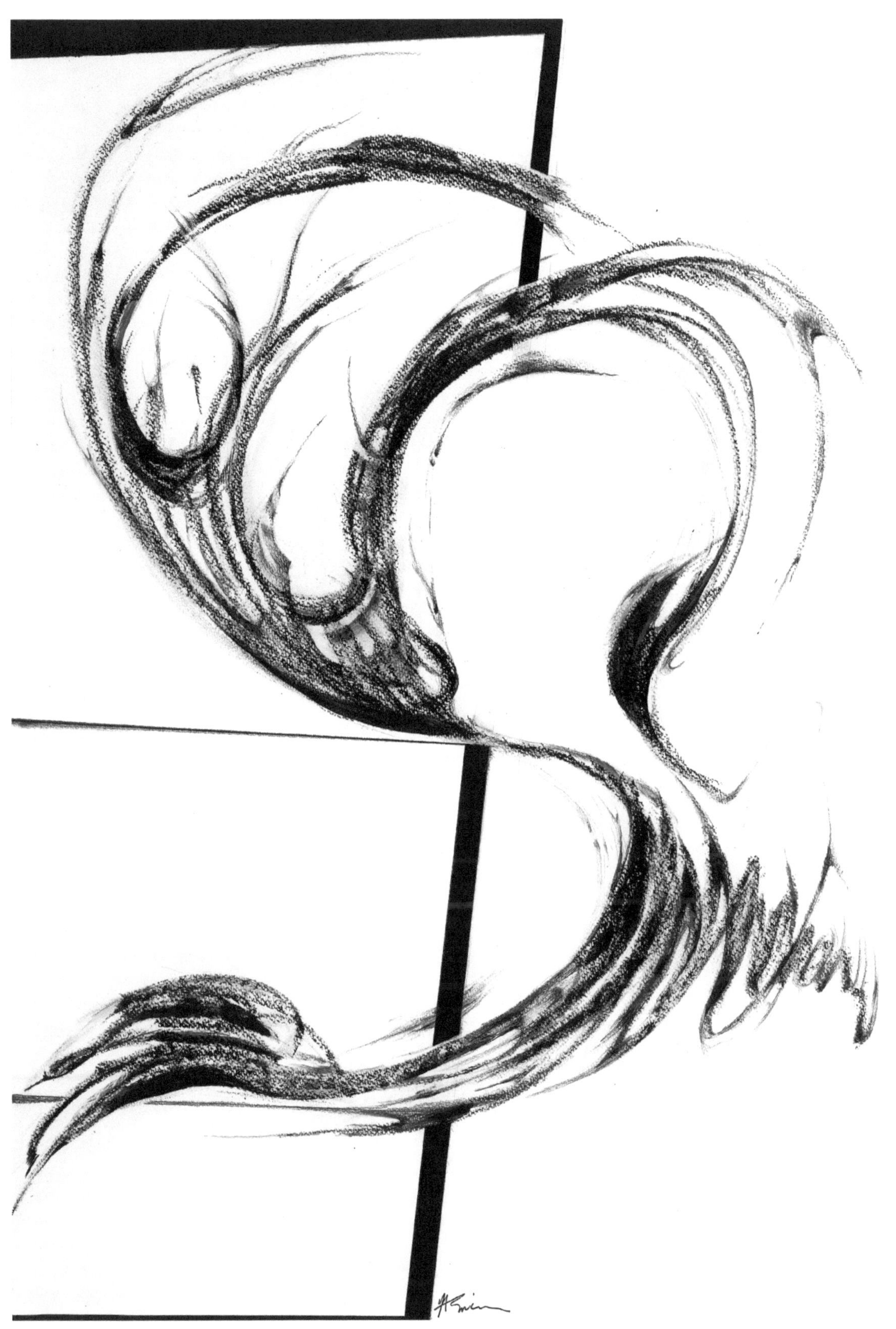

PLATE 48

Justice Flatlined

Wishes wash no dishes
Peace making
requires agency
requires belief in
the abolition of inequities

acrylic
24 x 36 inches

Page 120

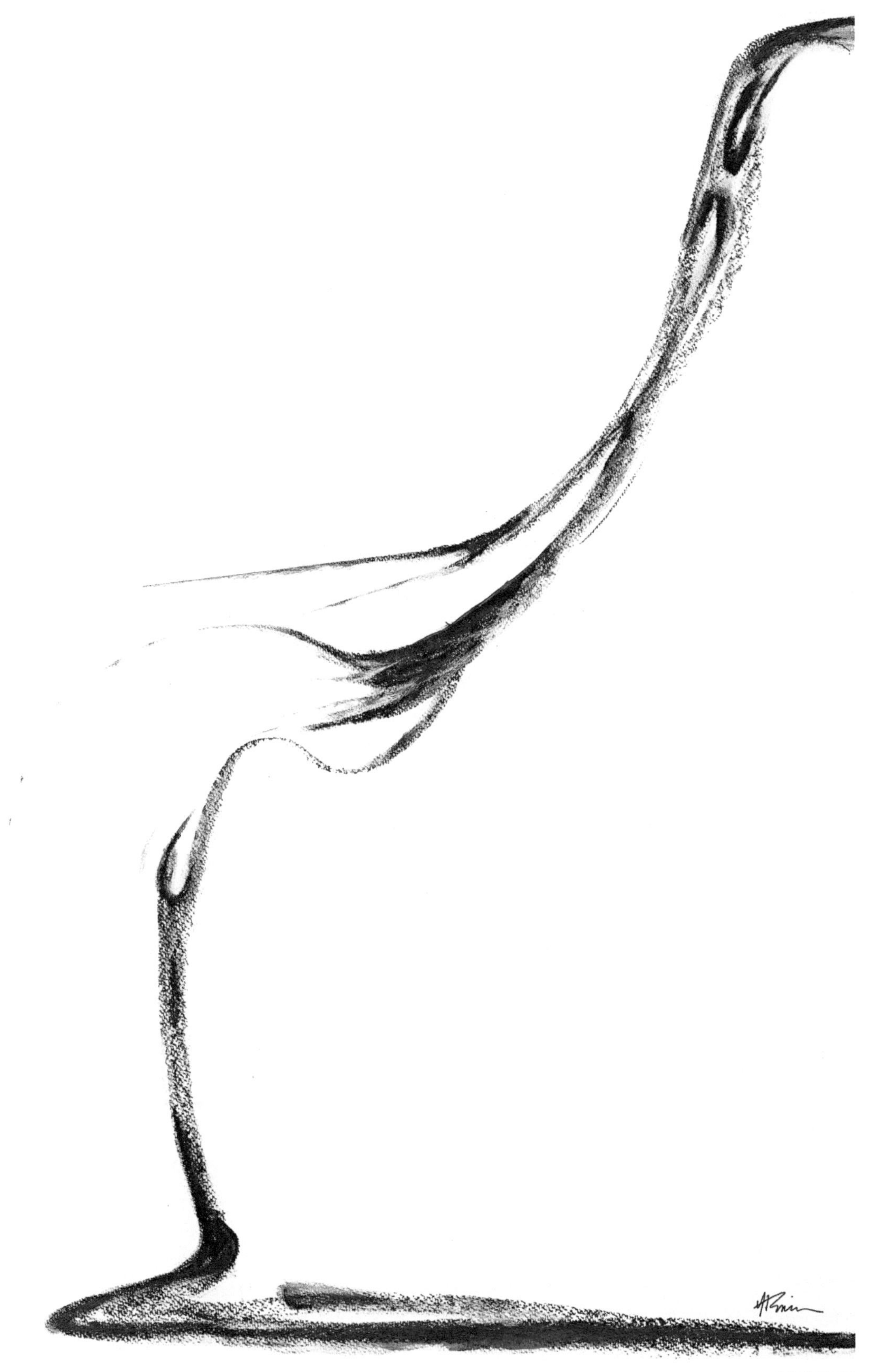

PLATE 49

Mother Grief

Precious are the lives of children
yours and mine
Grieving snatched lives
Cavernous and deeply felt
yours and mine
Hometown street and foreign soils
bewail the unnatural order

acrylic
17 x 33 inches

Page 122

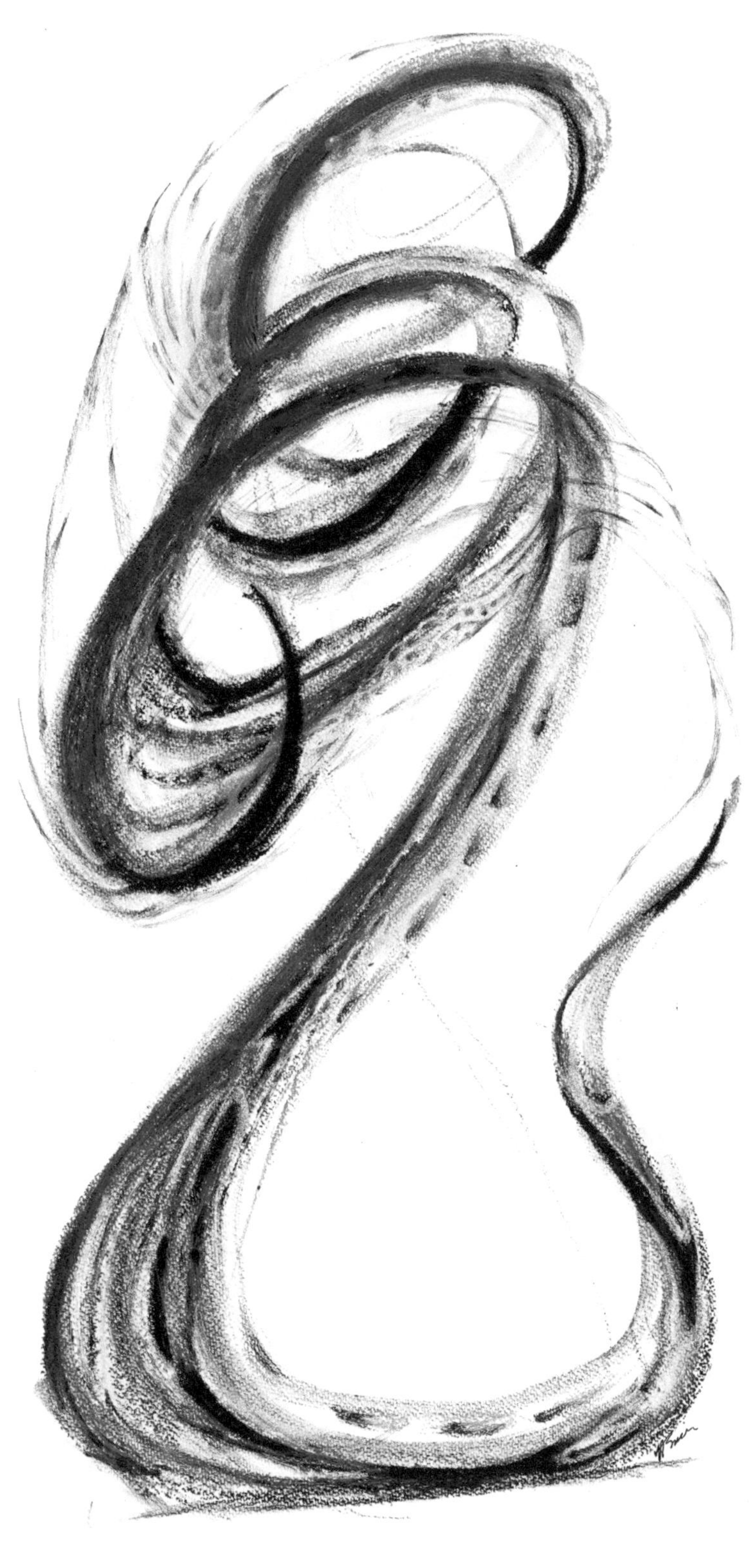

PLATE 50

We Are All Trayvon Martin

Disdain dignity
Assail body
Scrape humanity
Pierce soul
Done to one so is to all
Illusions surface roads
architected of avarice and hegemony

acrylic
17 x 33 inches

Page 124

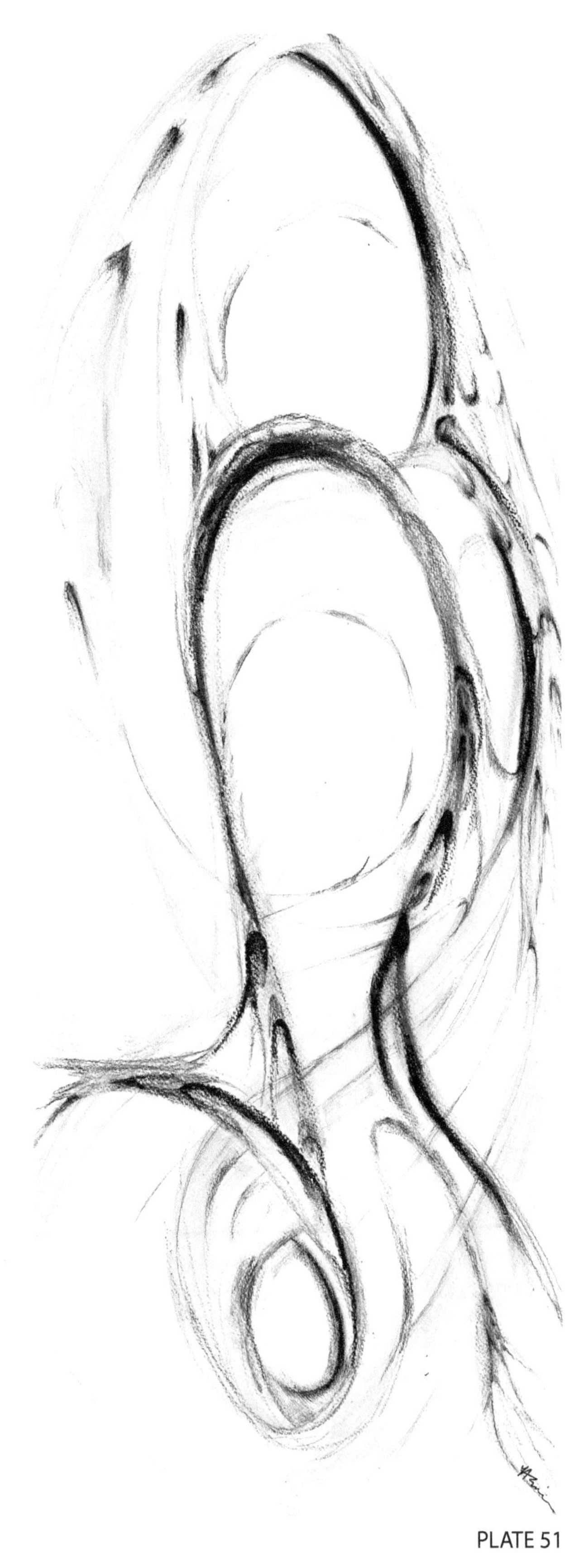

PLATE 51

Last Glance

Last glance taken when life was snatched
Future denied
Superiority presumed

acrylic
23 x 36 inches

Page 126

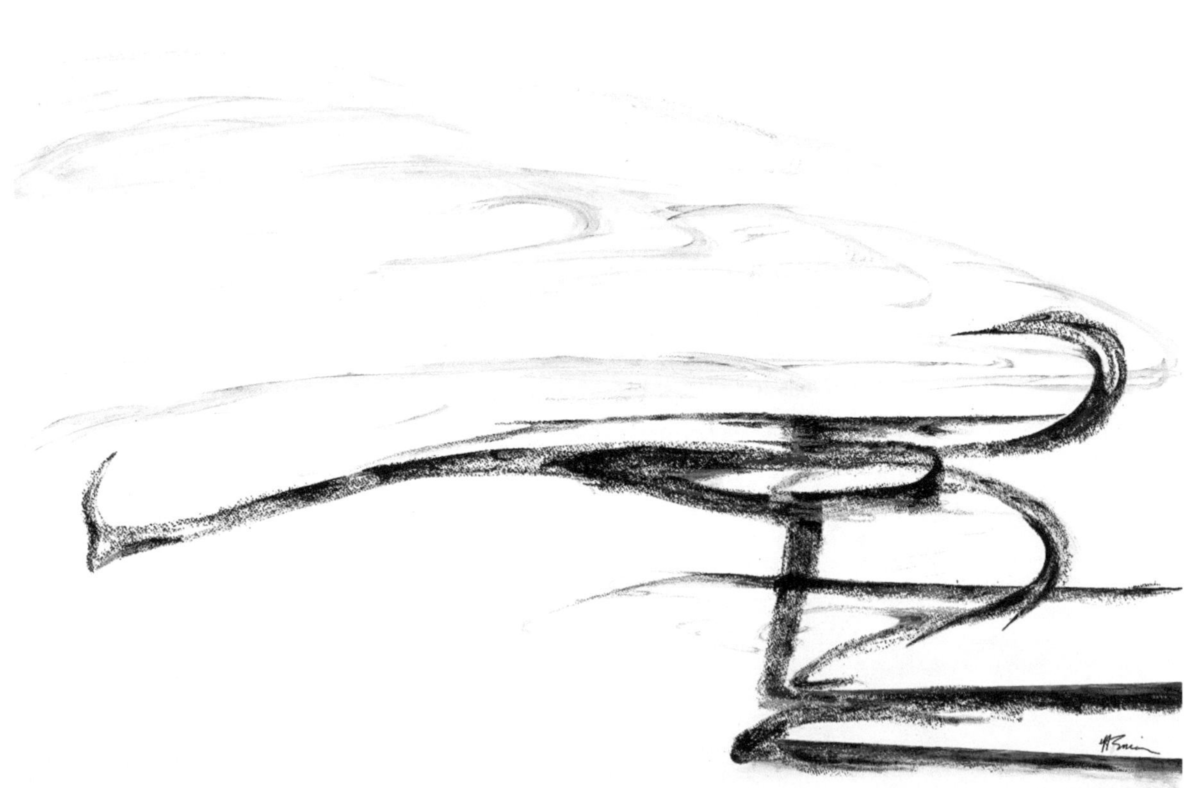

PLATE 52

Elusive

Wind glides mysteriously

Elusive seem the blueprints for decency
and intentional equity-making

Peace a deception
of shared lies fostering limited consciousness
and a debauched national conscience

acrylic
20 x 30 inches

Page 128

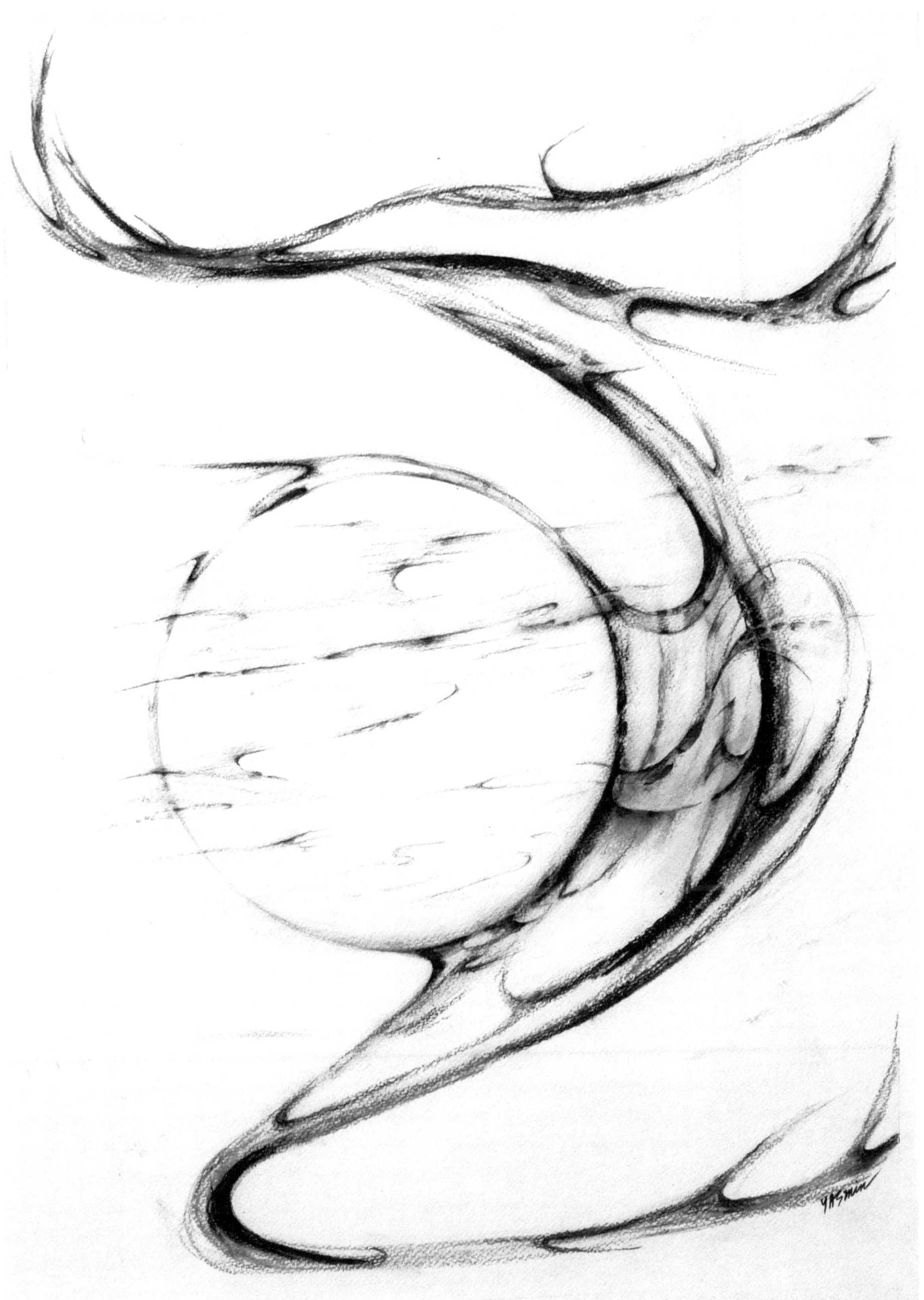

PLATE 53

Troubled Waters

Bringing to consciousness
a landscape of inequities and
troubled waters
that therein reside

acrylic and graphite
22 x 30 inches

Page 130

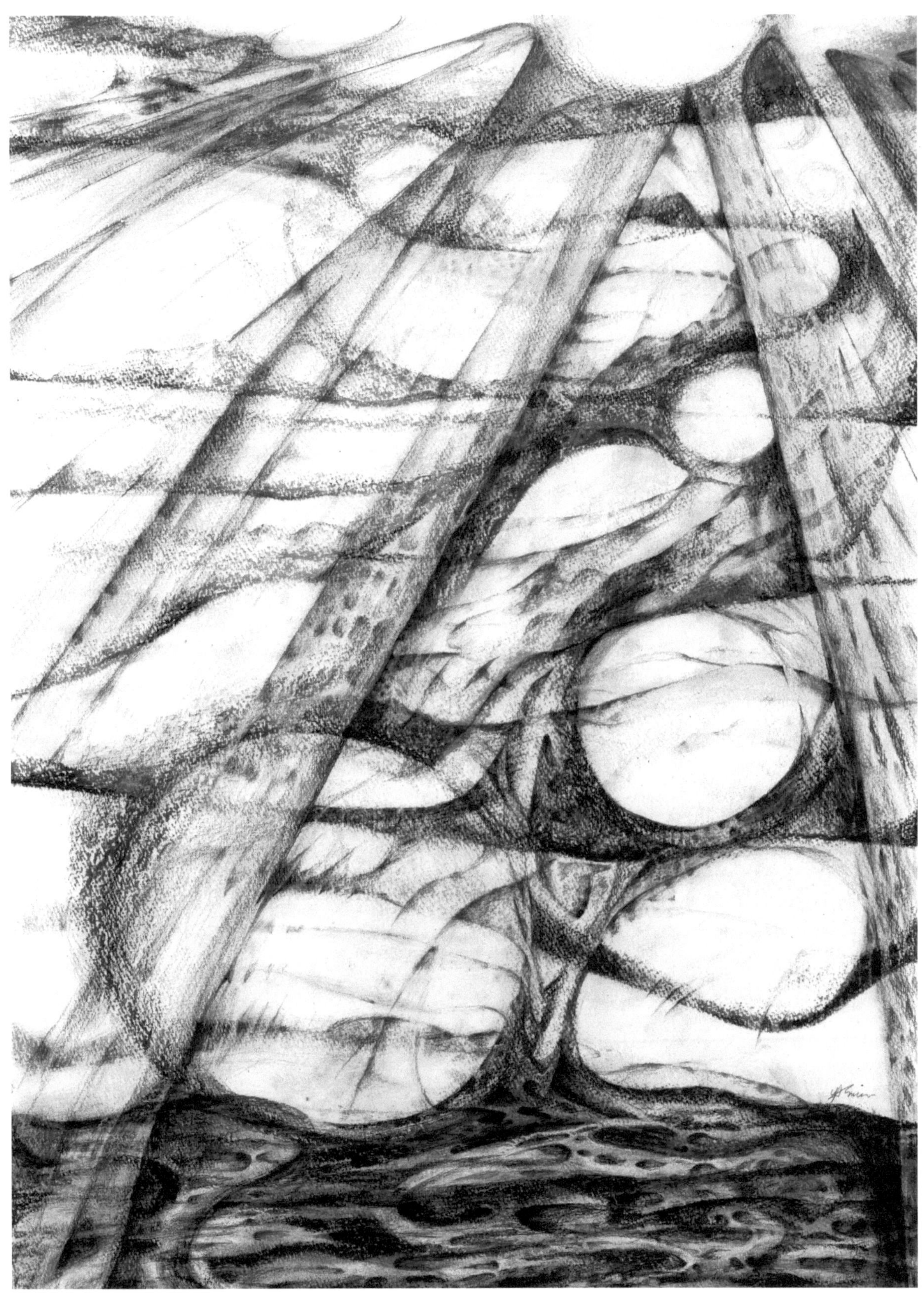

PLATE 54

Divergent Thinkers

Diversities of creativity
and intellect
nurture
landscape ecologies
tilling soils of potential

acrylic
22 x 30 inches

Page 132

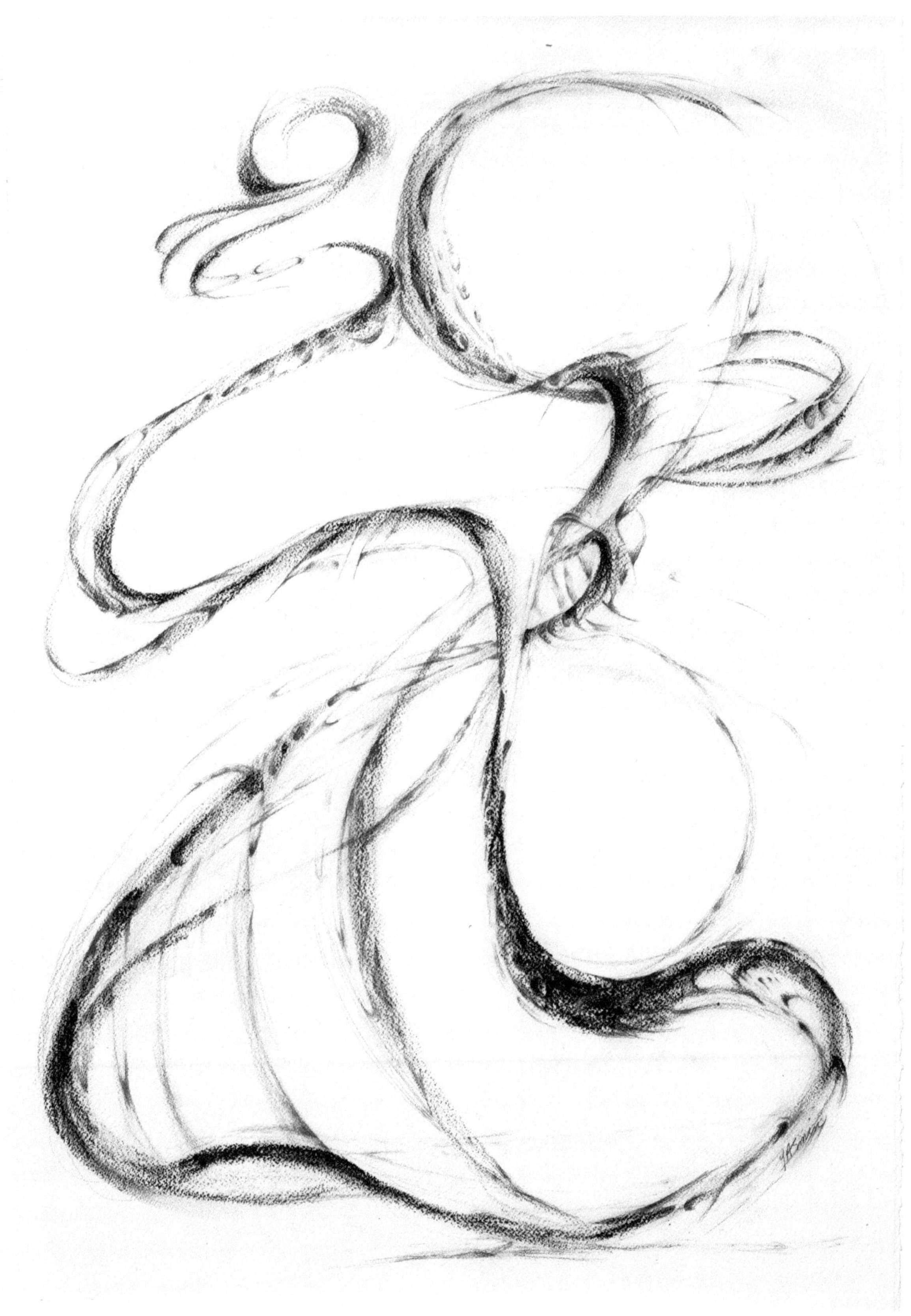

PLATE 55

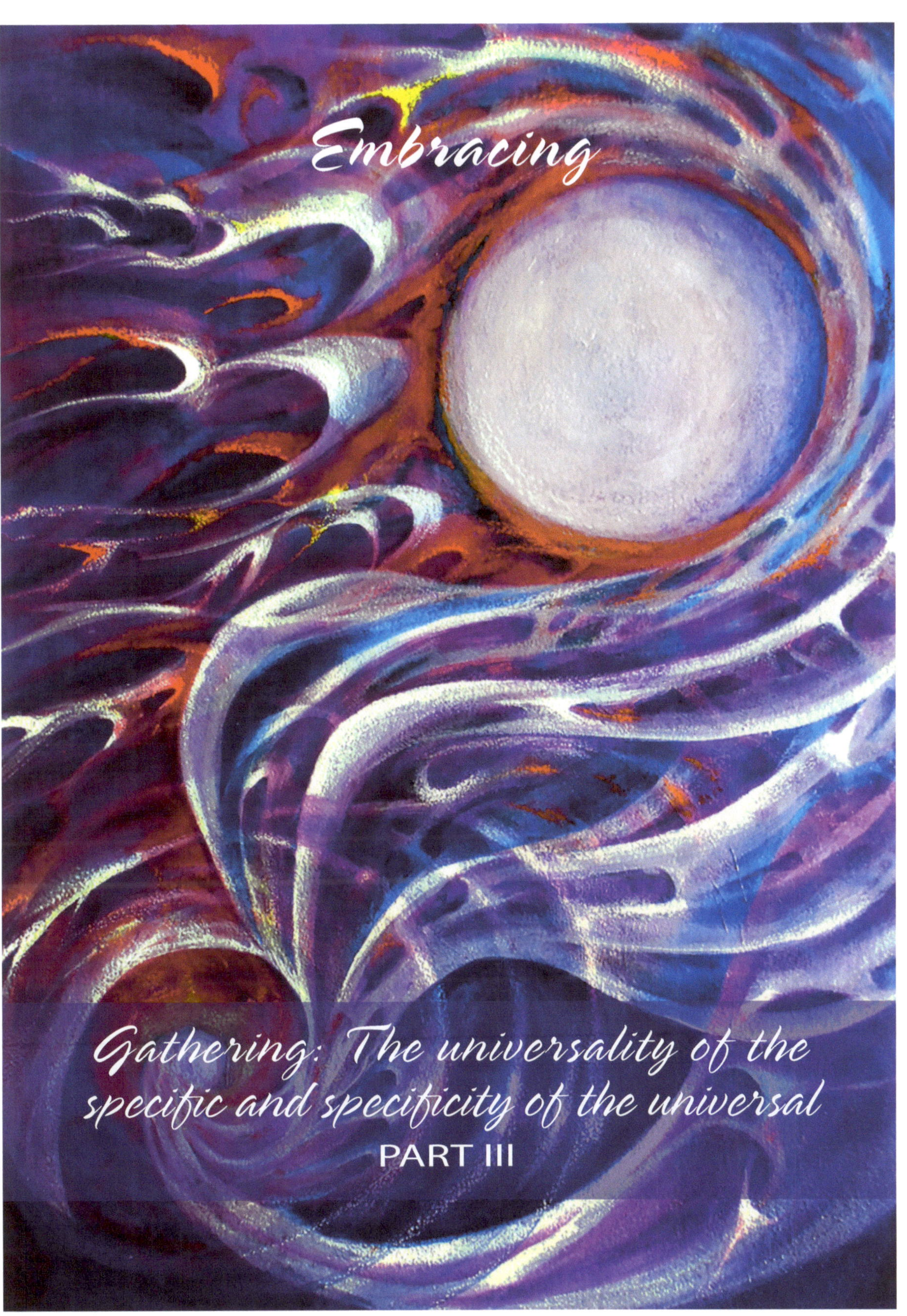
Embracing
Gathering: The universality of the specific and specificity of the universal
PART III

Embracing Oneness

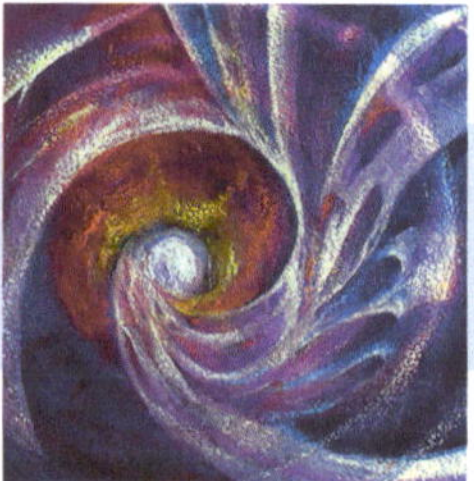 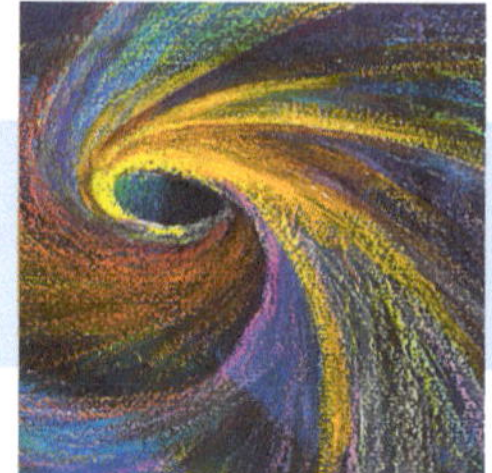 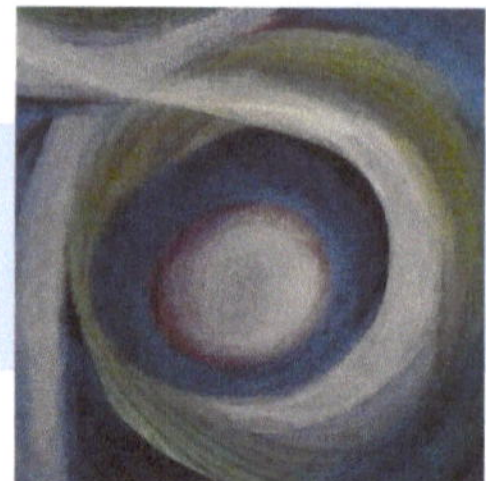

From my perch of view, oneness is the authorization and honoring of the intersectionality of sacredness. It is a dedication and celebration of epistemological, ontological and axiological diversity, including cultural, ethnic, linguistic, socio-historic and familial constructs, spiritual expressions, divergent perceptions, etc. I could not begin to speak of peace or happiness without bringing to consciousness that some people's peace and happiness are at the abject expense of others, thereby, rendering said emotional states, both unexamined and mitigated.

When I speak of embracing oneness, I am speaking of a cosmological indivisibility of all human and nonhuman elements. I am speaking of a call to action for us to step into our highest and best good; to hope, but not hope devoid of agency, yet with anticipation and vision holding towards peace wedded to justice. My paintings are calls to speak the truth about both wonders and injuries, and to resolve harm without involvement in reprisals, which ultimately damages all involved.

We may have been born into families that neither saw, nor honored our essence, or we might be in failed/failing marriages or partnerships—sometimes with great injury involved. We belong perhaps to communities, and subsets thereof that are despised and maltreated by dominating classes, or we may belong to targeted, marginalized and/or persecuted identity groups, etc. When we leave the offending familial configuration, win the hard won rights, or are liberated from oppression, we then sit at the precipice of possibly getting back at our tormentors, at punishing and retaliating against them for harms inflicted.

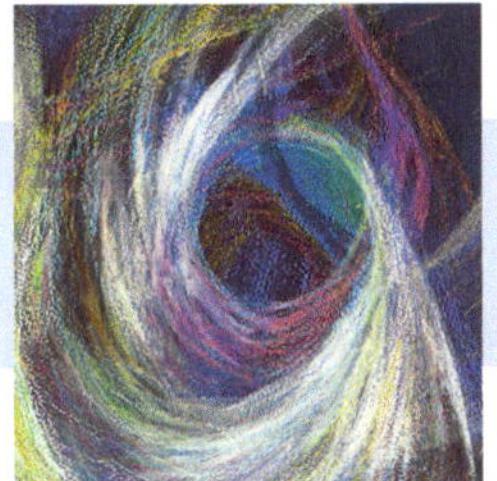 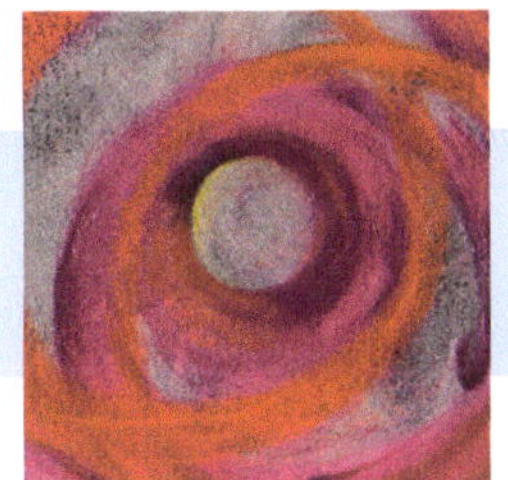 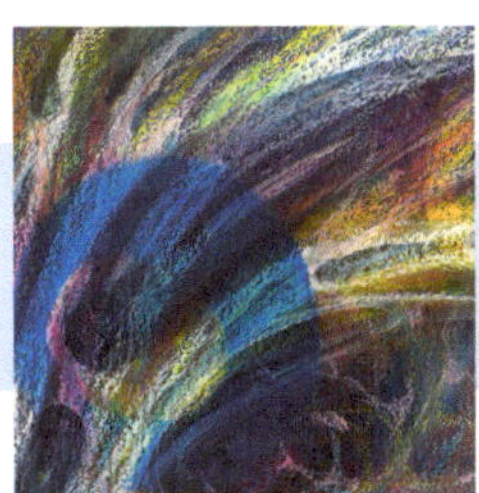

When, however, we choose to retaliate, we then join in a convoluted dance of wasted lessons, of invitations for circuitous suffering, and one of depriving ourselves and generations to come of potential models for mindful accountability of offenses without needs for revenge.

In the US, we tend to be a punishment-oriented society; hence, we have huge prison industrial systems; we imprison the mentally ill; we incarcerate youth for nonviolent and status offenses and often end up releasing angry youth trained mostly to later claim a cell in adult penal systems. We imprison without treatment, without rehabilitation, without education, without reconnections to people, spirit and nature … and we imprison with class and color-coded justice. Such patterns of punishment produce self-masticating like cycles of recidivism and multigenerational fodder of wasted potential.

Our propensity to punish has taken intra/interpersonal tolls in terms of gang development, rising youth and young adult suicide, rising familial, school and community violence commingled with rampant institutional abuses, which position us for the dismantling of participatory democracy. It further feeds an ever-expanding pattern of intergenerational poverty, wedded to an oligarchic government steeped in debauched national and international practices. We sit in need of a social justice movement. The arts can illumine a journey towards health and wholeness.

My visual and poetic images are a call for social consciousness, and a call for connections to *Spirit*, —not to religion, but to the essence of the spirit of doing only that which we would gladly invite back into our own lives and those of our loved ones. My collection stands as a call for art and socio-political activism, for the enlivenment of walking in integrity, decency, and courage to stand up for what we know to be truthful and life affirming.

Universal Specificity

The specificity of the universal adores the
universality of her specifics
Meandering boundaries of souls
at once
minute and infinite,
at once
part and whole

acrylic and oil pastels
22 x 30 inches

Page 138

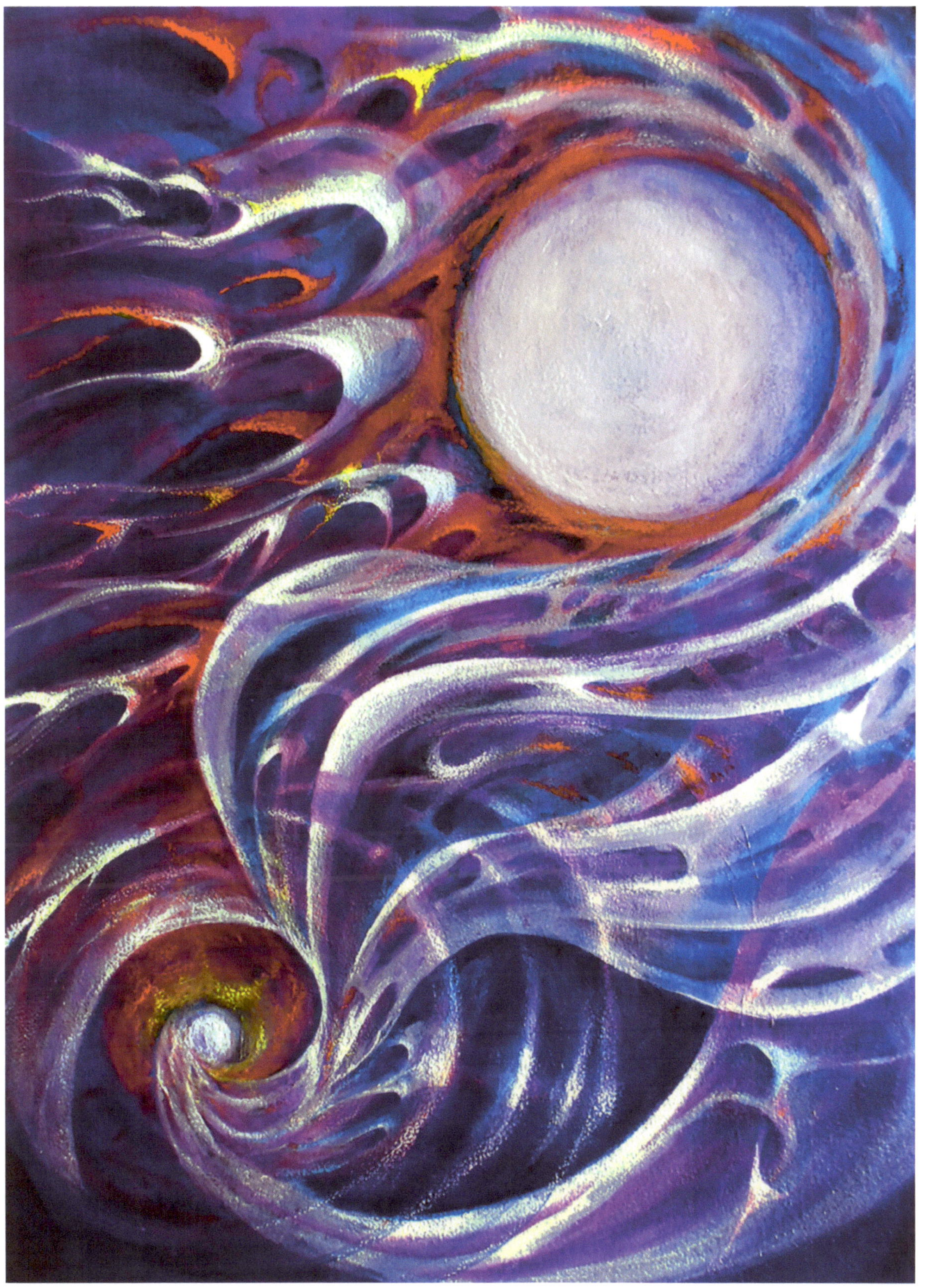

PLATE 56

Mystery

The unknown, known
Unseen, visible
Inside, inseparable from outside
I am
that I am

acrylic
10 x 10 inches

Page 140

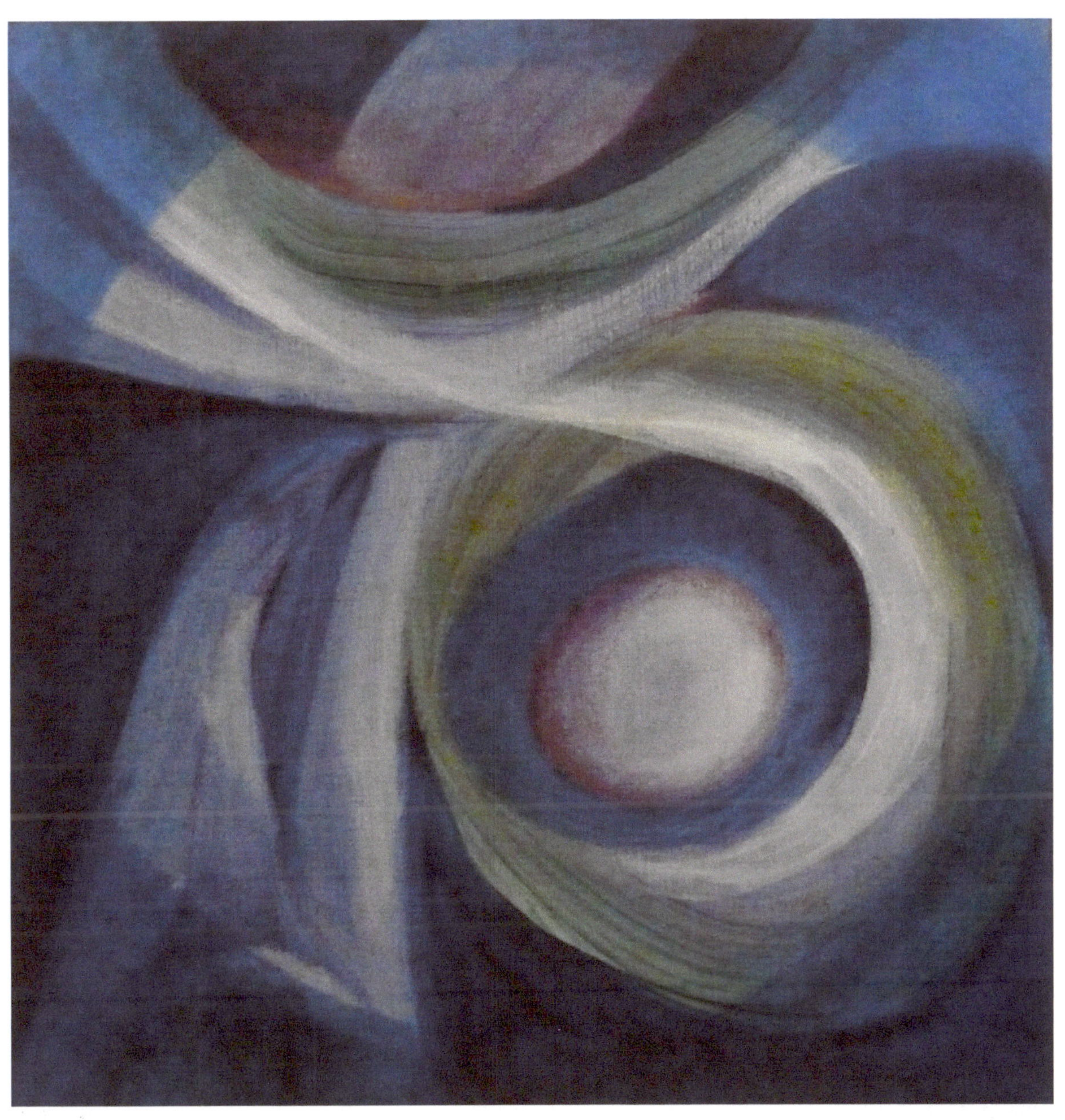

PLATE 57

Seeking Oneness

Seeking
inseparability
of polarities
until they are one

Oneness as the indivisibility
of life's sacredness
and the quality afforded therein.
Happiness, peace and *Spirit*-honoring cannot
reside in authenticity if its residence is built on
the necks of the marginalized *other*

acrylic and oil pastels
22 x 30 inches

Page 142

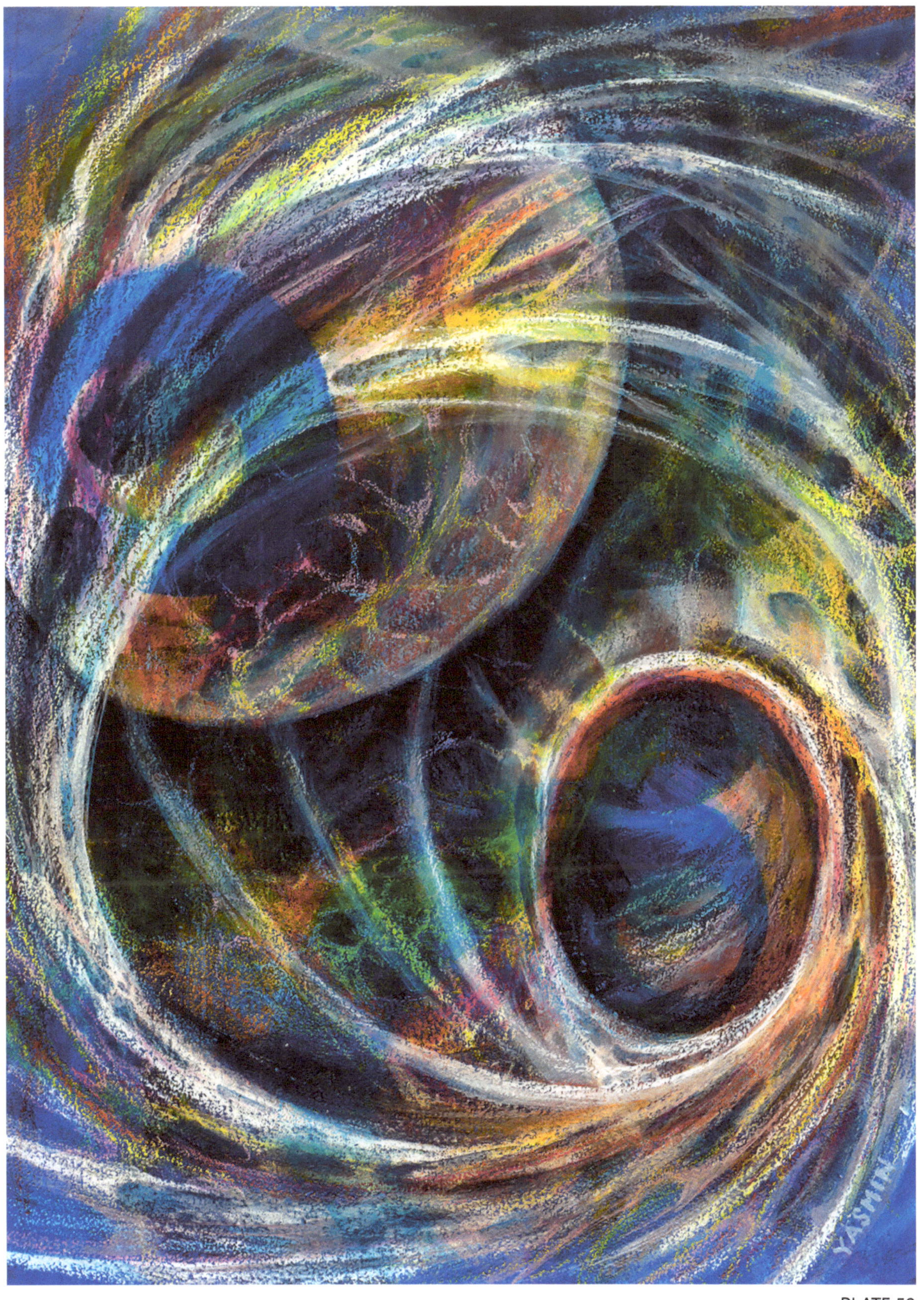

PLATE 58

Mother and Child

Wearing faces of ancestors
carved in landscapes of perception
Mine,
and in their time,
theirs

acrylic and oil pastels
22 x 30 inches

Page 144

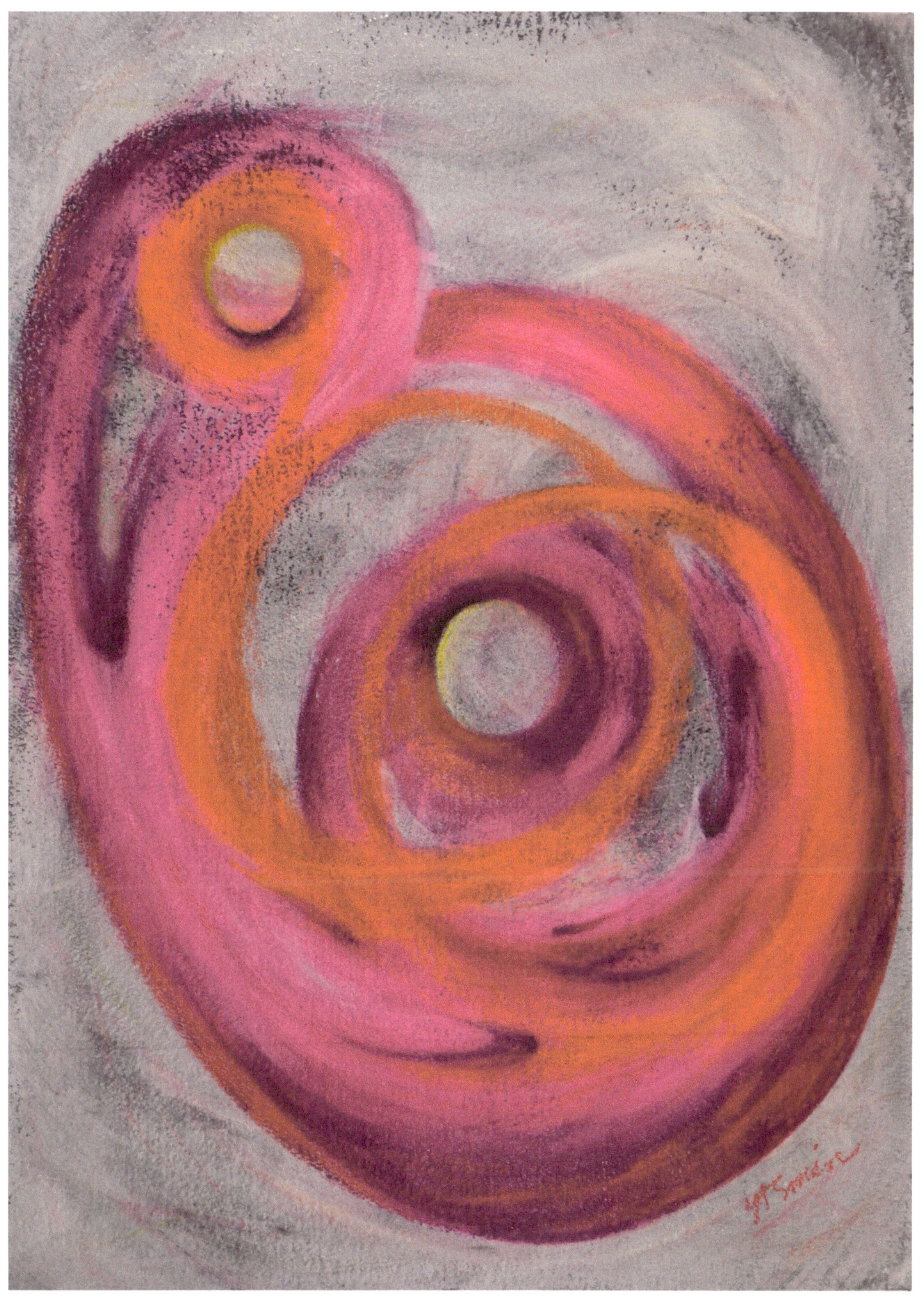

PLATE 59

The Dance

Knowing
realities without words
The practice
of experiencing
joy

acrylic and oil pastels
22 x 30 inches

Page 146

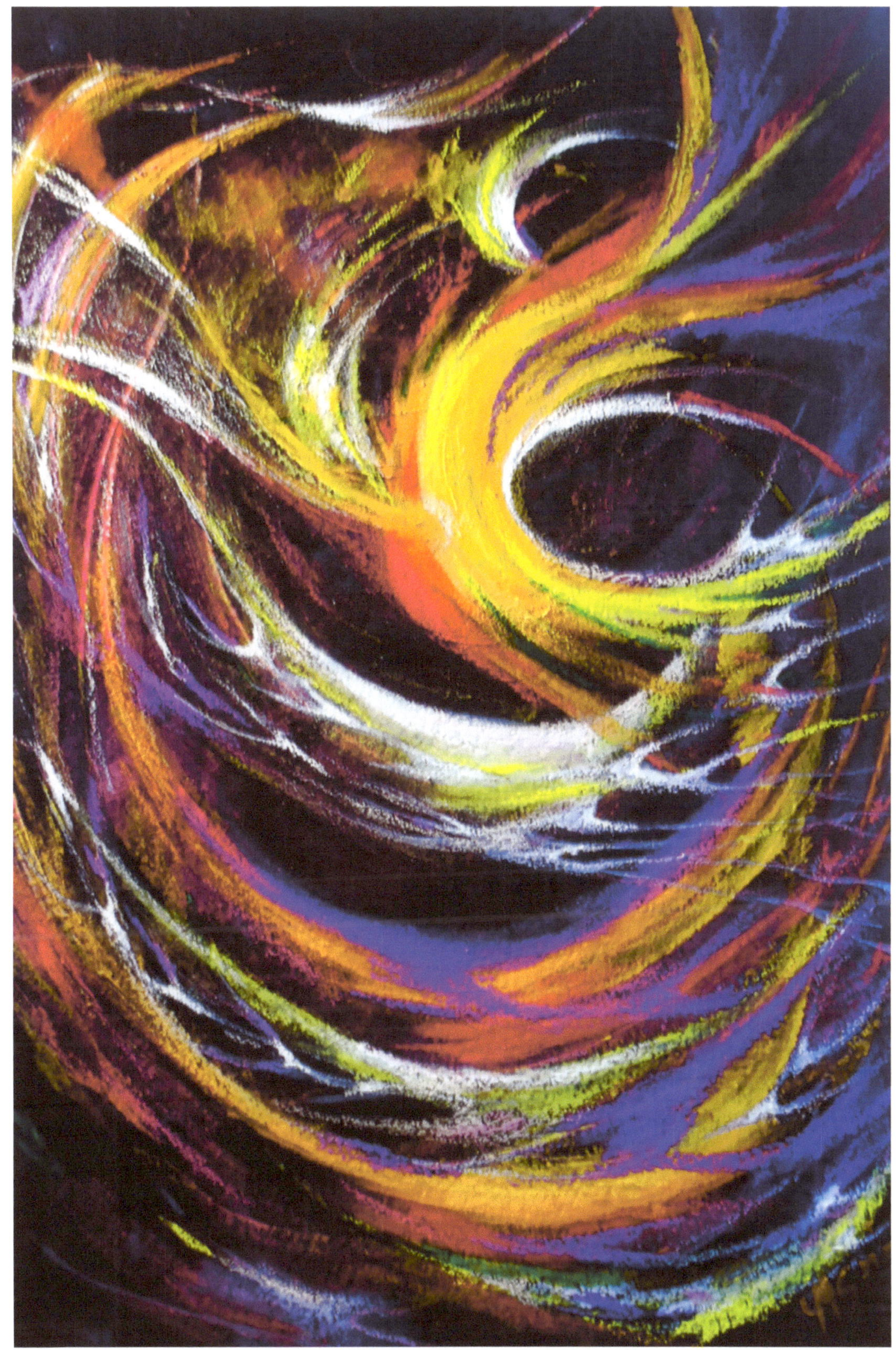

PLATE 60

Seeds of Joy

Tenderness awashed
germinates splendor
sprouting
toward
blooms of delight
and forms thereof

acrylic and oil pastels
22 x 30 inches
collection of Penny Shrawder

Page 148

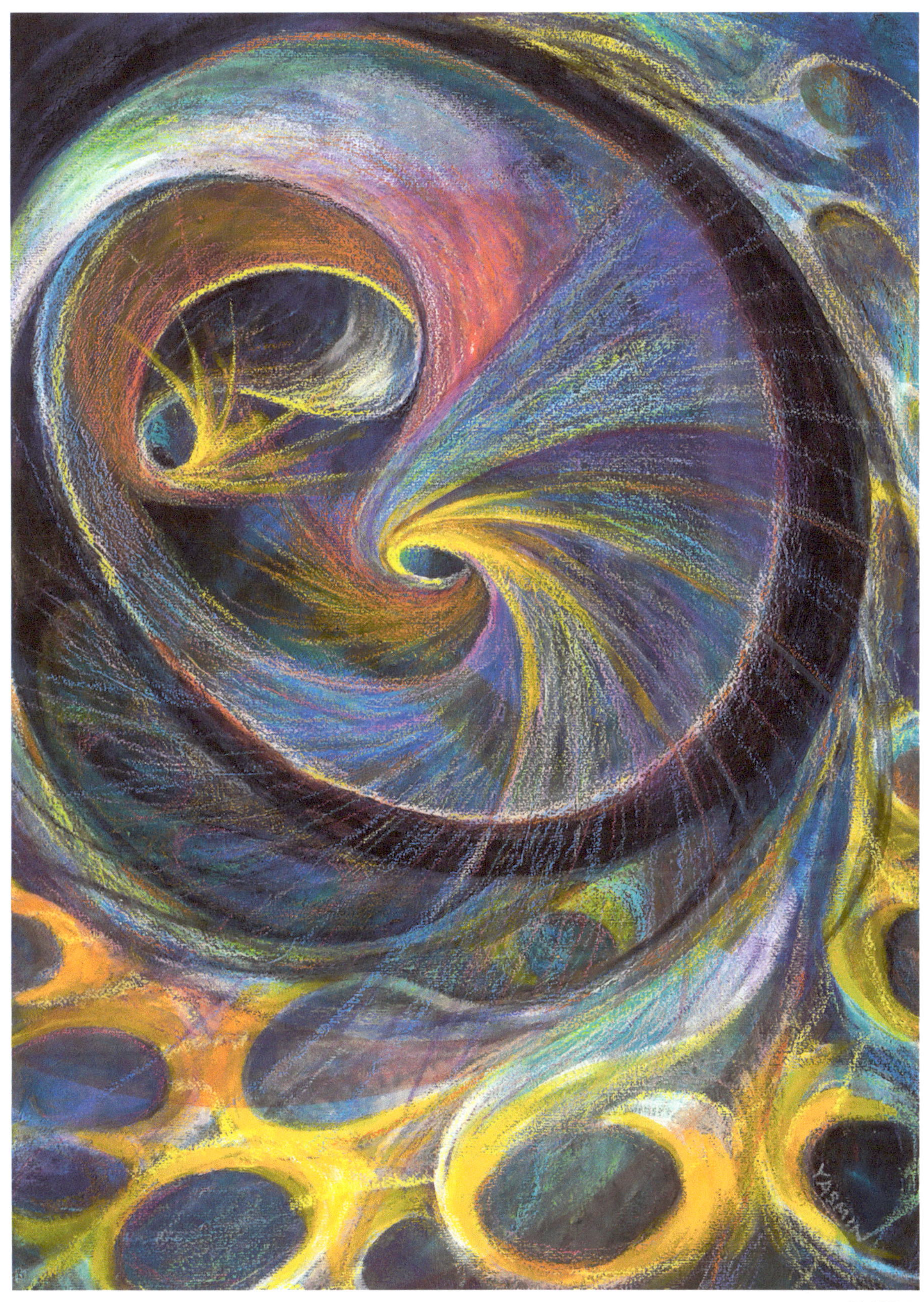

PLATE 61

Embracing Hope: Vision Holding

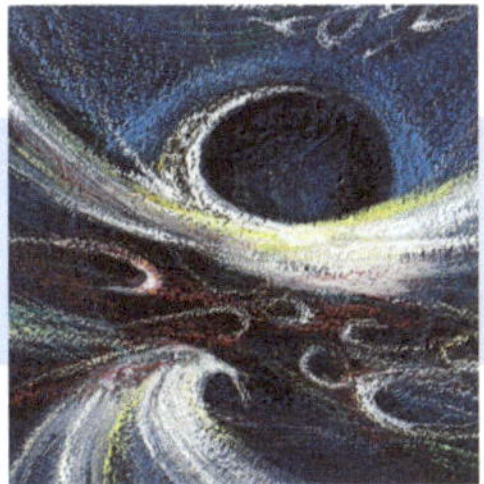

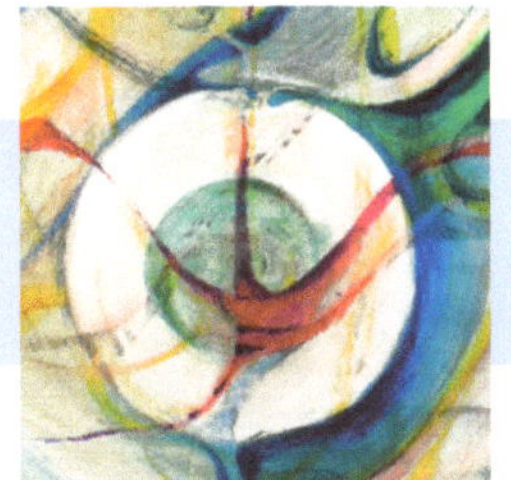

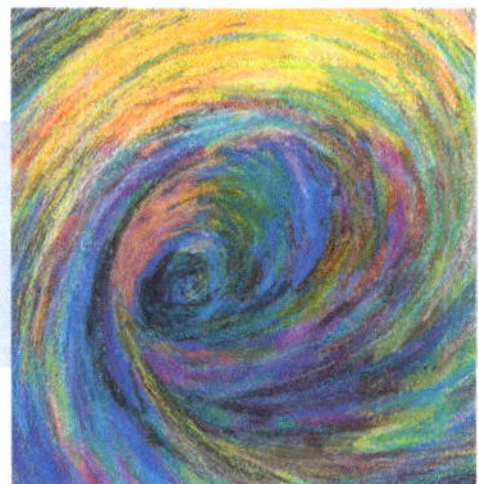

If a human being did not have an eternal consciousness, if there were no sacred bond that knit humankind together … how empty and devoid of consolation life would be.

—Soren Kierkegaard

There is no passion to be found in settling for a life less than the one you are capable of living.

—Nelson Mandela

In my lens of perception, hope is about an anticipation of wholeness for humanity. It is a supplication for peace wedded to justice. Dr. Martin Luther King, Jr. is cited as defining justice as, *love correcting that which revolts against love.* Inequities revolt against wholeness; however, embracing a vision of inclusivity, a philosophic framework of omnipartiality and commitments to change both self and society, valorizes hope inside and out.

Hope inspires my rising in the morning
Visits my tongue and consciousness
urges pen to hand and paint to brush
Spreading beliefs of restorative justice
and consciousness of reconciliation without reprisal
flourish hope
Emanating whispers of righting injustices
individual and historic
matures hope
Hope nourishes agency, and agency hope in return
And so I rise, awakened with expanding anticipation
of limitations arching towards opportunities to sit at the table of inclusivity
in awe and honoring of the sacredness of creations
and the earth that supports us all.

Power Without Apology

Claiming personal power in the countenance of commonly held opinions of women of African ancestry as: too big, too loud, too opinionated, too aggressive, too bossy, too much, too much too much.

acrylic and oil pastels
22 x 30 inches
collection of: H. Gail Rucker

Page 152

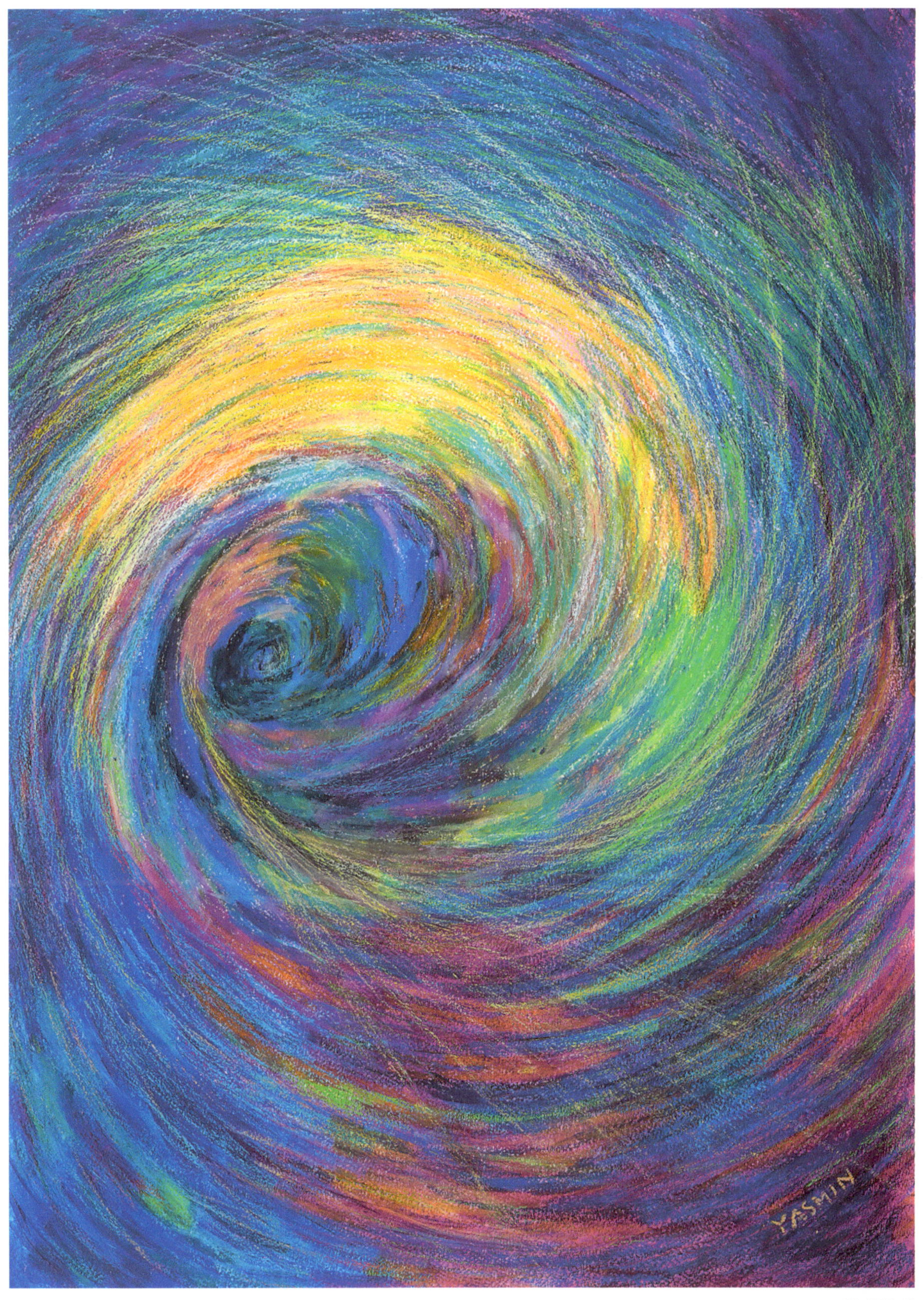

PLATE 62

Happiness

Individual and materialistic
happiness
hollow joys
Eudaimonia
more significative
than hedonistic satisfaction
yet unexamined
dims grandeur and value
of both
and robs hope its place

acrylic
22 x 30 inches

Page 154

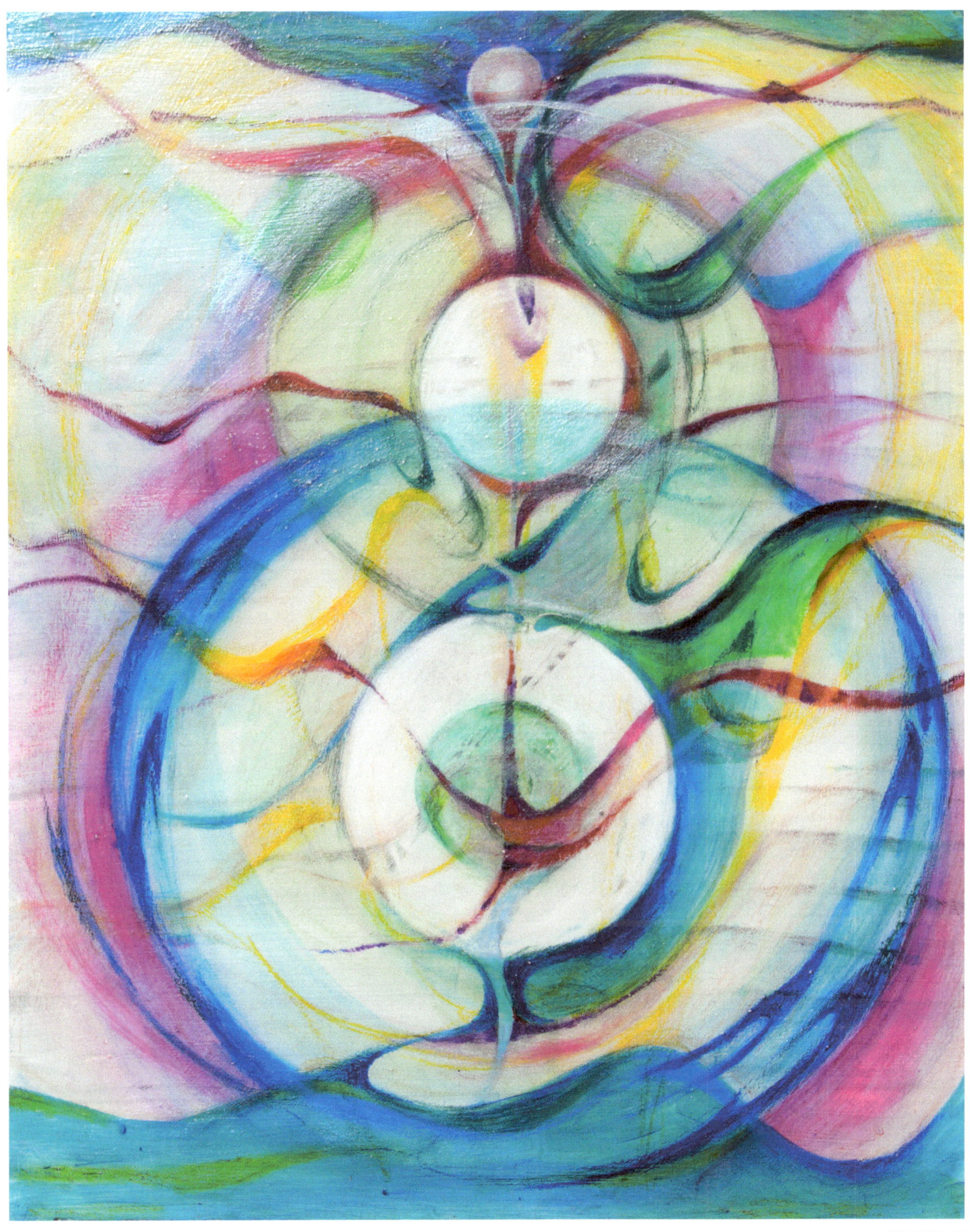

PLATE 63

Intentional Shifts

Beliefs held
mindfully and purposefully changed.

It is said, that things that have had life often struggle to maintain its breath, even outdated and no longer useful ways of perceiving existence.
When we understand that we can make intentional shifts in our own lives, we create space that the same might be true for others.

acrylic and oil pastels
30 x 22 inches

Page 156

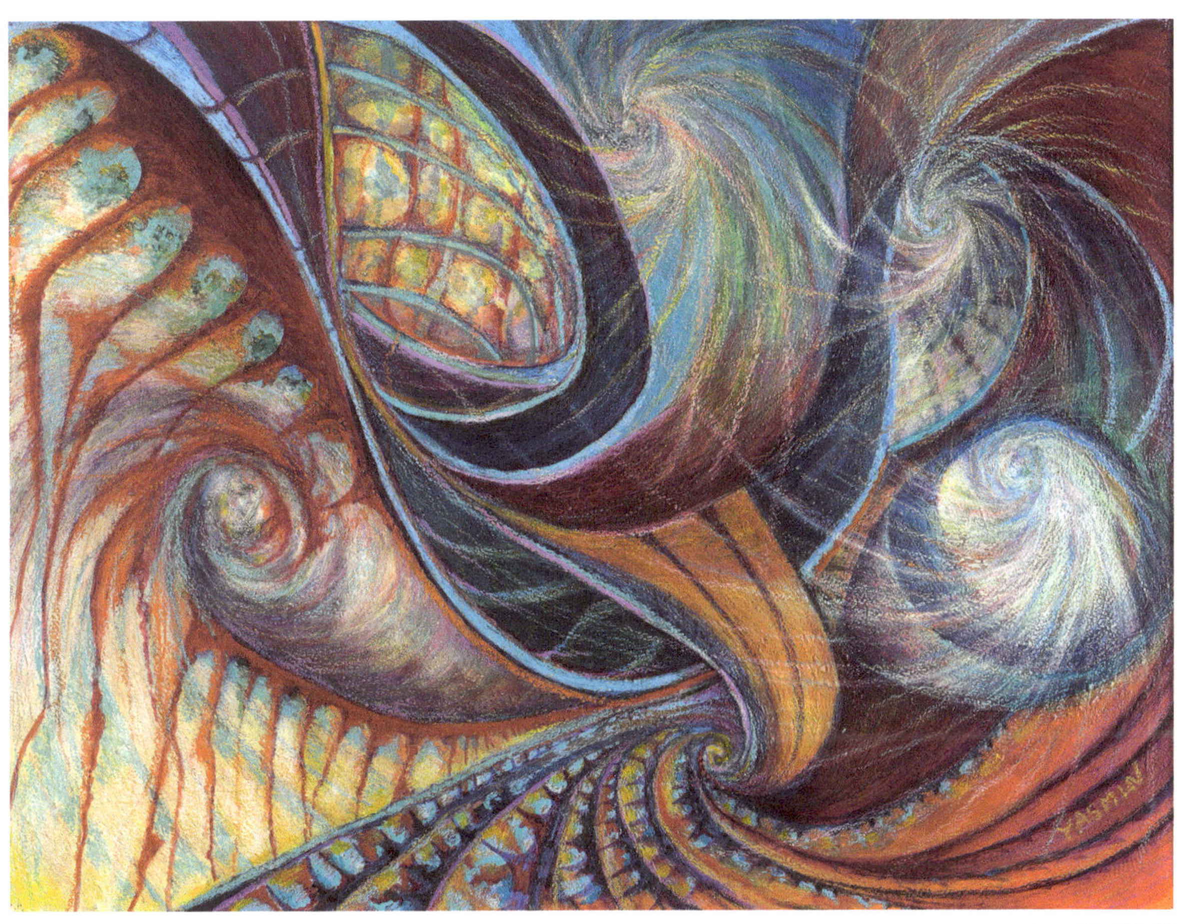

PLATE 64

Hope

With hints of bergamot and oranges dancing on her breath,
she comes in mid of night whispering the long of wait,
the long tarrying for reclamation of self, gone in amnestic stillness.

With notions of freedom, and particular veins of hope
and uncertainty
she calls for us to vision across divides
beyond prisons of limitations
towards prisms of opportunities,
no matter the bend of light

acrylic and oil pastels
22 x 30 inches

Page 158

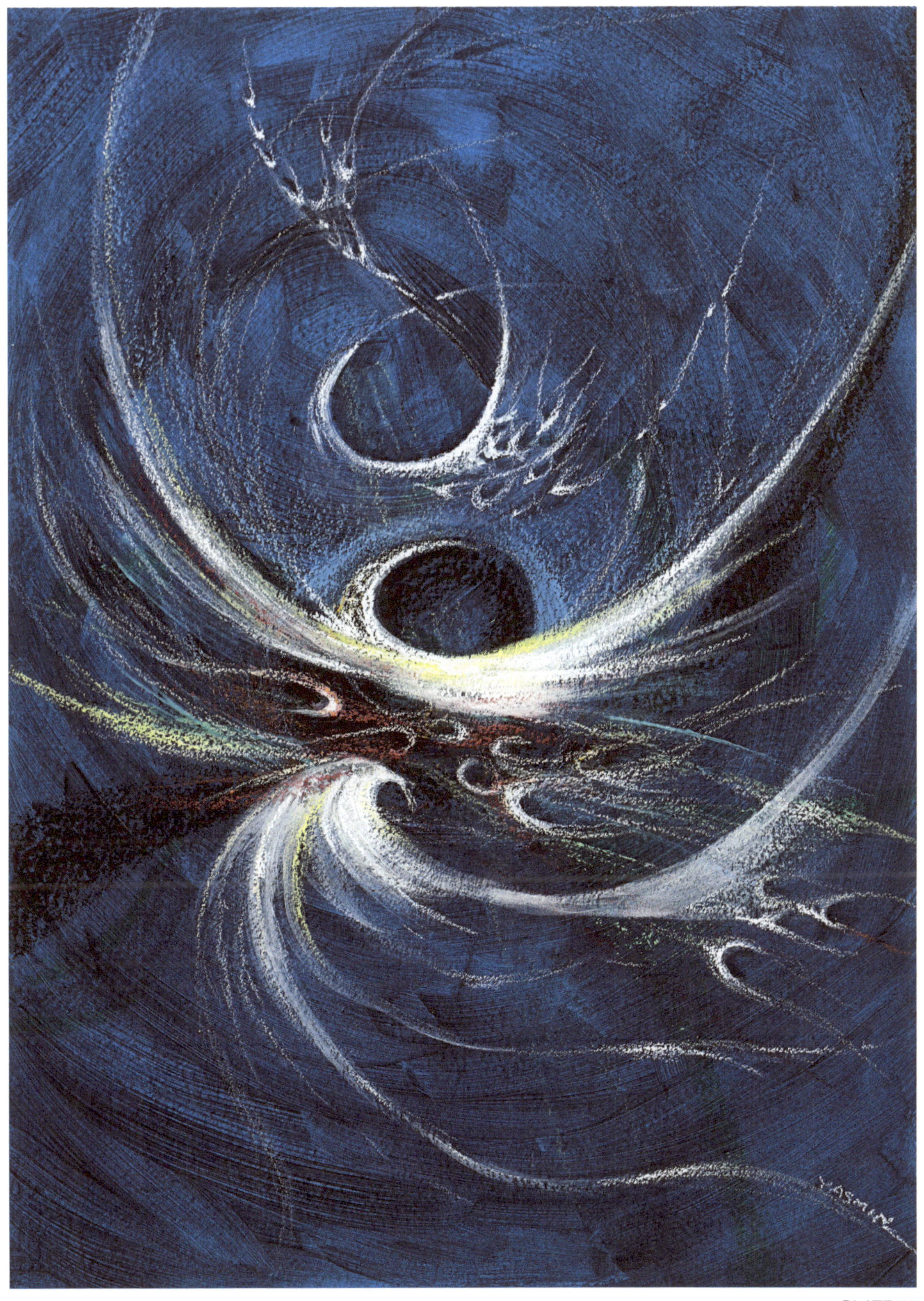

PLATE 65

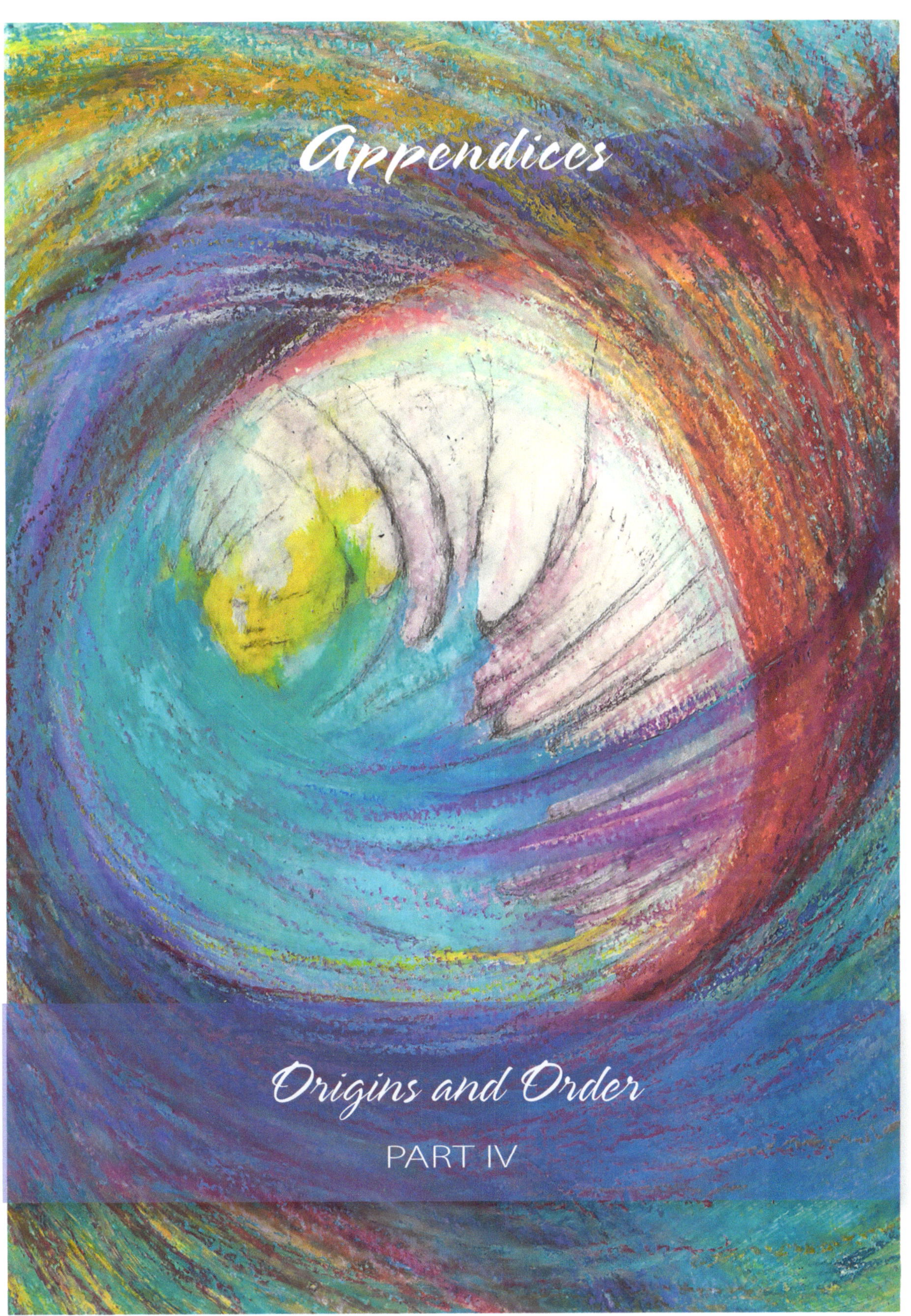
Appendices
Origins and Order
PART IV

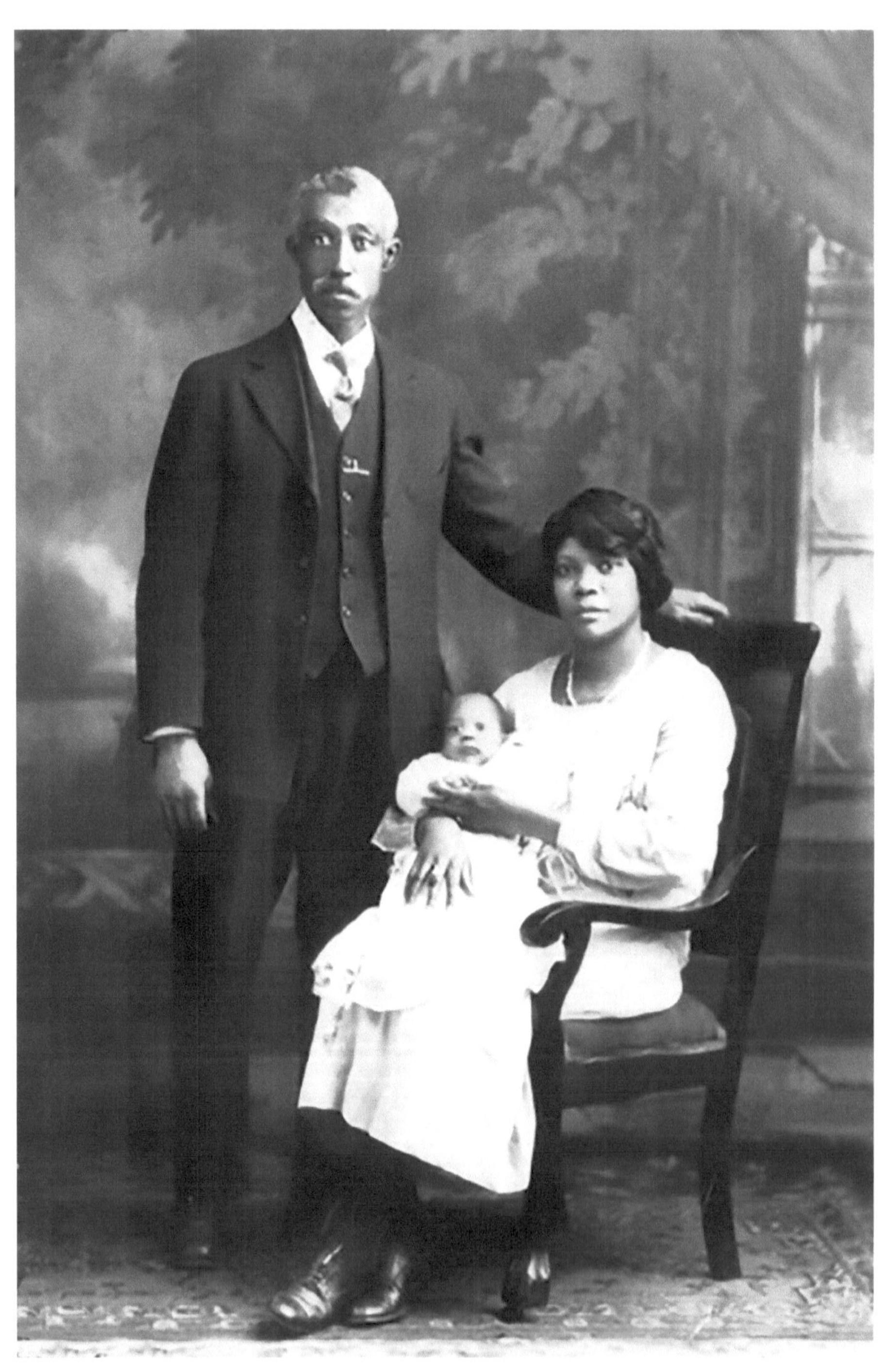

Grandpa and Nana, 1926

My Family

In my family, I occupied the middle position of five children, and today sit in the middle position of five generations of living in the US (immigrant grandparents, parents, my generation, my children's and grandchild's).

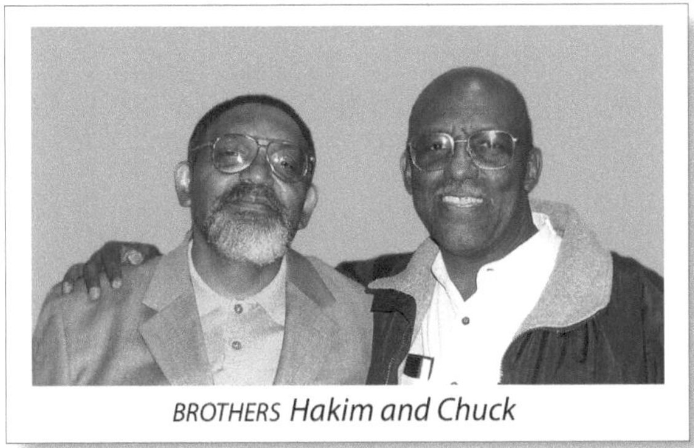
BROTHERS *Hakim and Chuck*

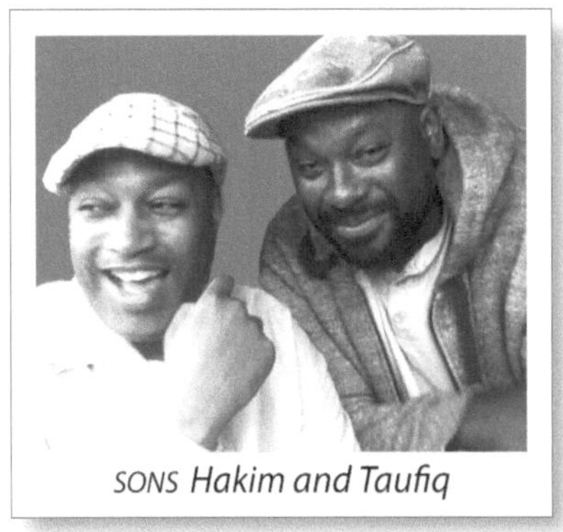
SONS *Hakim and Taufiq*

I imagine my brothers, *Big* Hakim and Chuck, feel connected in the special ways that brothers often do. My sisters, one older, one younger, knew me in ways as no other could claim. The sudden loss of my sister—eleven months my senior—in many ways was deeper, more painful and emotionally discombobulating than the loss of my parents. I often wonder what might have become of Kim had she not died at 31 years of age.

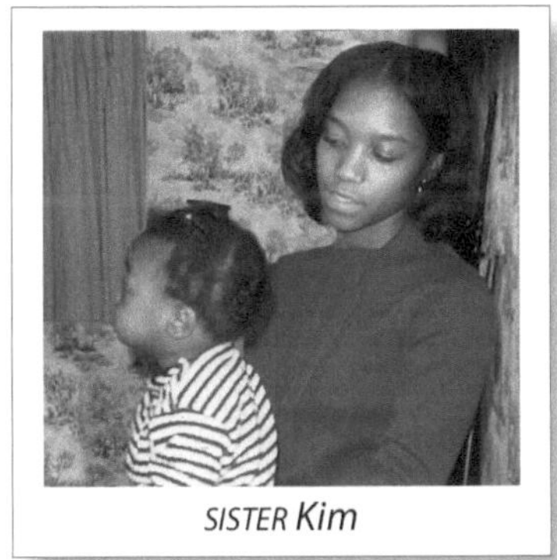
SISTER *Kim*

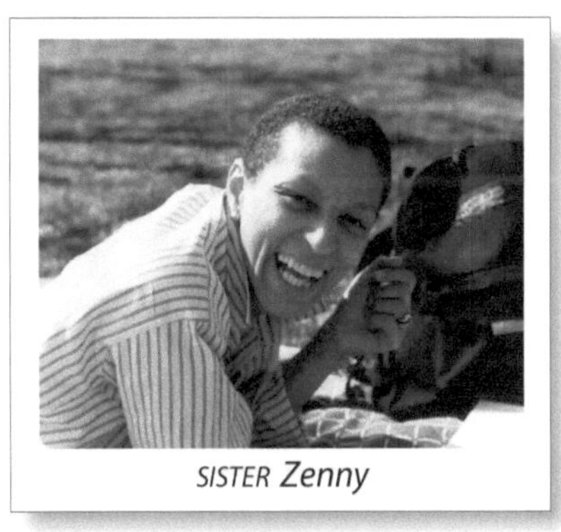
SISTER *Zenny*

My sister—six years my junior—is my best friend in this world. Zenny's unswerving living-love of *Spirit* is of the highest caliber. How she walks in honor and integrity, and love leaves footprints on the journey that I am proud to walk along, in the greatest of tenderness. Both my brothers are deeply spiritual in very different ways, and both their ways guide their feet and make them whole.

I was married young, and for almost a dozen years. We were way too young, and way too traumatized by life and war to create a healthy and enduring relationship. We are, nonetheless, friends some forty-eight years later. Melvin and I made two sons, laid one to rest following a fatal motorcycle accident, and have one grandchild. We are family.

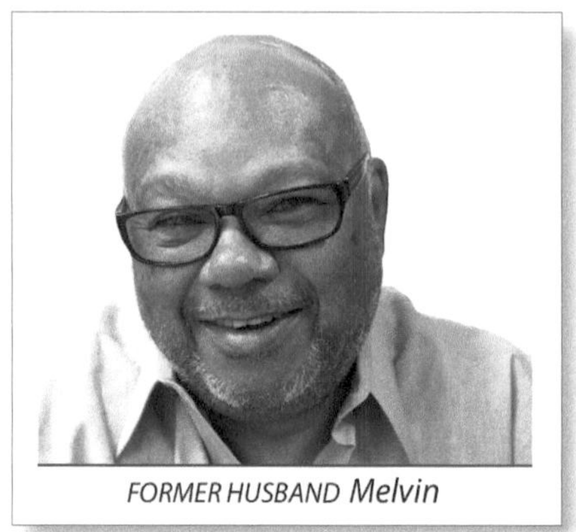

FORMER HUSBAND *Melvin*

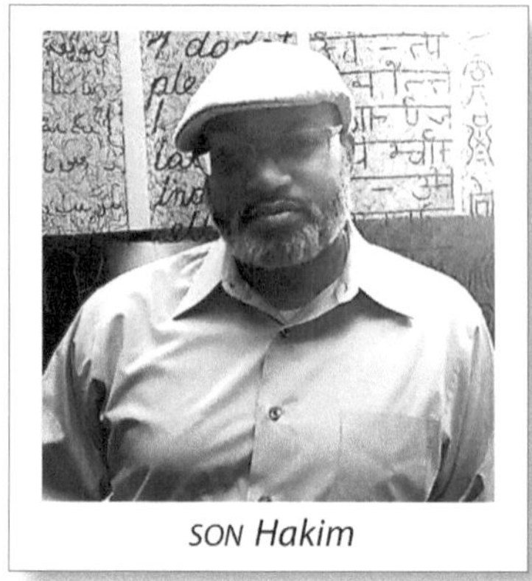

SON *Hakim*

My firstborn, Hakim, stands as a renaissance person in his array of brilliance: visual artist, writer, musician, chef, computer nerd, intellect … and all commingled with notable integrity, and clarity of politics. My love for him has no bounds. Hakim and his brother, Taufiq, bonded one to the other in remarkable ways and probably more deeply than he to his parents.

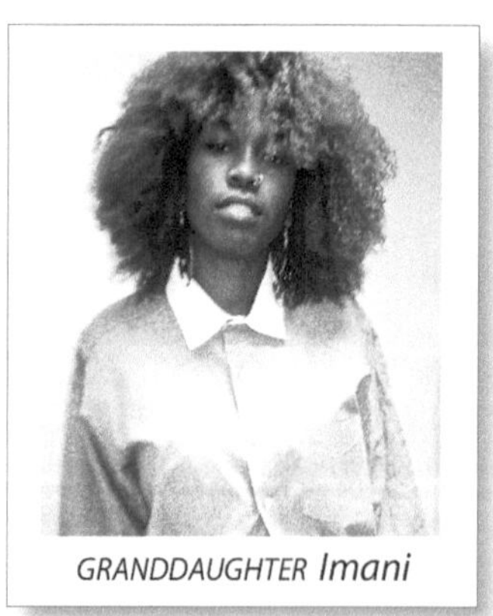

GRANDDAUGHTER *Imani*

Imani, my granddaughter, now a young woman, an artist and blossoming social critic said she knew little grief until she lost her father. His death turned her life upside down. When she was a youngster, she knew everything about everything in ways that some children do when they know they are valued. Watching her articulate belief systems that are rooted in theory and values inspire hope, pride and adoration.

I spent my formative years living with my grandparents, who were 90 and 60 years of age at my birth and both of whom lived to be centenarians. They hailed respectively from Cabo Verde (small islands off the west coast of Africa), and the Caribbean island of Jamaica. Although they had hegemonic, colonial educations, their primary lens of perceptions remained more ethnic than not. They graciously lent their eyes to me, so I could see the world.

Perhaps it is the immigrant tale of cultural traumatization for the first generations of newcomers. My family did not escape a journey marked by the traumas of coming to the US as educated immigrants only to be met with Jim Crow laws and segregation.

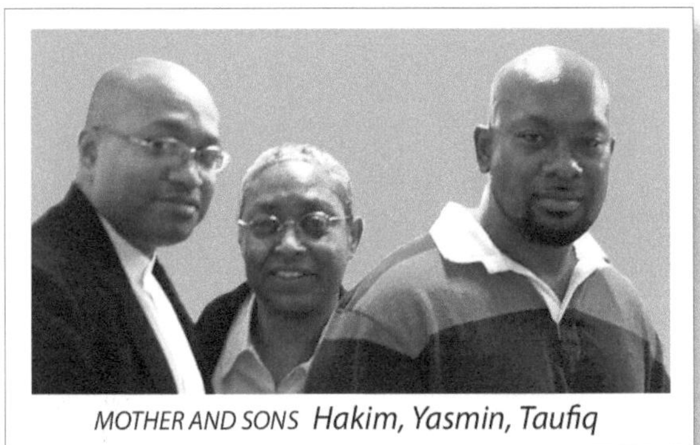

MOTHER AND SONS *Hakim, Yasmin, Taufiq*

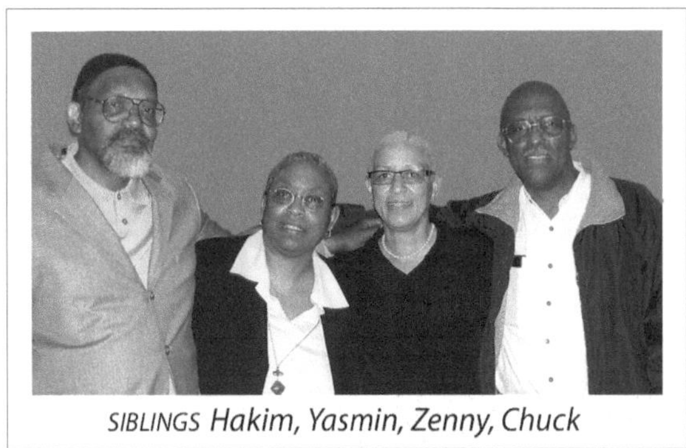

SIBLINGS *Hakim, Yasmin, Zenny, Chuck*

My grandmother's brother, Amos, was a civil rights worker before there was a civil rights movement. He was a Carnegie of Jamaica. He was beaten severely many times. His advocacy informed my political consciousness, but embarrassed my mother who wanted nothing more than to simply assimilate in US culture.

In this country, especially when I was young, there was precious little space allowed for cultural diversity within the diasporic African community. Hence, Black people from the Caribbean, from Africa, from Latin America ofttimes struggled with identity, and ofttimes after a few generations, stopped identifying with the cultural roots they brought to Ellis Island. I struggled.

From a young age, I struggled with an American identity, with the hypocrisy of freedom and justice for all. I struggled with a childhood neighbor saying, even in his army uniform, he had to ride in segregated train cars, with my uncle's severe beatings, and later my own. Belonging became an existential issue, and although greatly diminished, remains today.

With untied tongue, I claim the entirety of my familial lineage and entirety of experiences. I thank them for the solid backs, sturdy shoulders, borrowed eyes and many life lessons.

Index of Plates

Watch Night Bird: Looking out for freedom

In the historically rooted Black American church, Watch Night Service is a New Year's Eve gathering, first held on December 31, 1862. There, many enslaved Africans in US confederate states anxiously awaited the arrival of Emancipation Proclamation into law.

This image is in acknowledgment of the watching out for that specific liberatory agency, and symbolic of all those watching out for release from injustices.

watercolor ink
24 x 18 inches
collection of Leah Rescate

Page 168

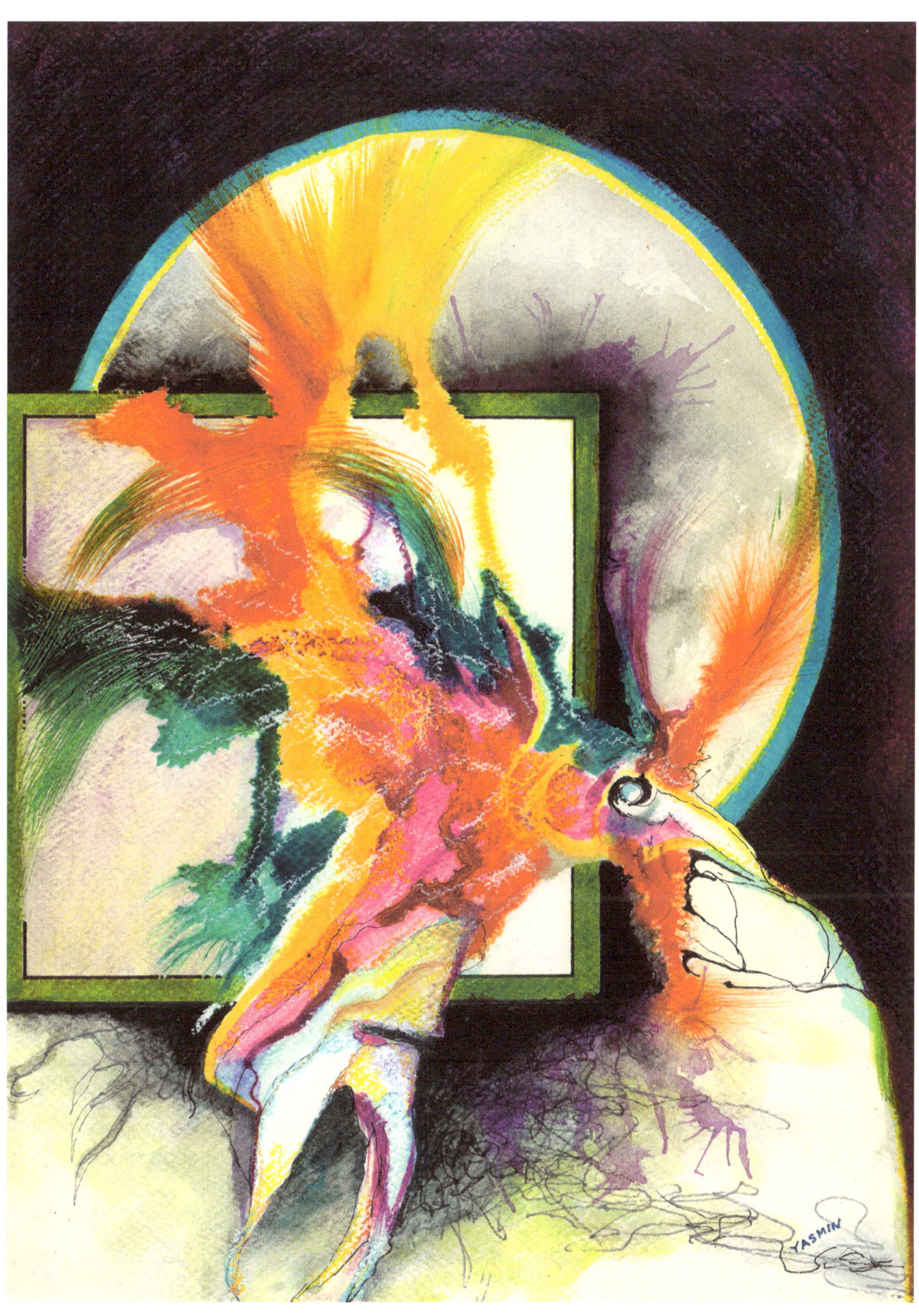
YASMIN

Visit my website

Fonts used throughout this book are
Myriad Pro and Spring LP

www.ingramcontent.com/pod-product-compliance
Lightning Source LLC
LaVergne TN
LVHW070121110826
845147LV00002B/164

* 9 7 8 0 9 7 4 0 9 1 5 3 2 *